SDK228 The science of the mind: investigating mental health

Core concepts in Mental Health

This publication forms part of the Open University course SDK228 *The science of the mind: investigating mental health*. The complete list of texts that make up this course can be found at the back. Details of this and other Open University courses can be obtained from the Student Registration and Enquiry Service, The Open University, PO Box 197, Milton Keynes MK7 6BJ, United Kingdom (tel. +44 (0)845 300 60 90; email general-enquiries@open.ac.uk).

Alternatively, you may visit the Open University website at www.open.ac.uk where you can learn more about the wide range of courses and packs offered at all levels by The Open University.

To purchase a selection of Open University course materials visit www.ouw.co.uk, or contact Open University Worldwide, Walton Hall, Milton Keynes MK7 6AA, United Kingdom for a brochure (tel. +44 (0)1908 858793; fax +44 (0)1908 858787; email ouw-customer-services@open.ac.uk).

The Open University, Walton Hall, Milton Keynes MK7 6AA

First published 2010

Edited and designed by The Open University.

Printed in the United Kingdom by Bell & Bain Ltd, Glasgow

The paper used in this publication is procured from forests independently certified to the level of Forest Stewardship Council (FSC) principles and criteria. Chain of custody certification allows the tracing of this paper back to specific forest-management units (see www.fsc.org).

ISBN 978 1 8487 3690 0

2.1

Contents

Chapter 1 Explanations in mental health

Frederick Toates

1.1 Understanding mental health and ill-health

Welcome to SDK228 *The science of the mind: investigating mental health.* SDK228 is concerned with investigating, and therefore understanding, the causes of mental health and ill-health and applying this knowledge to understand and critique the treatments and interventions that exist for mental health disorders. This first book explores some basic principles associated with an understanding of mental health and ill-health, setting the scene for the topics of the books that follow: *Mood and Well-being*, *Addictions* and *Dementias*. It does so in terms of brains, minds, behaviour and social context, starting with the illustration of some cases of mental health and ill-health. Chapter 1 introduces the basic principles underlying the nature of explanations in this area and how such explanations are constructed. Chapter 2 then presents enough information about brains and minds for you to be able to form an understanding of mental health and ill-health by linking events in the mind to events in the brain. As you will come to understand throughout SDK228, this relationship between mind and brain has served a key role in the development of treatments for mental disorders and underpins much of medical thinking about mental ill-health. Chapter 3 gives examples of phenomena of mental well-being and the kinds of explanation that can be brought to bear on them by linking mental events, brain events but also social context in an integrated perspective. Finally, Chapter 4 looks at the vexed issue of how professionals go about diagnosing when someone is experiencing a mental illness and what kind of diagnosis is given to it.

In the cases of mental illness that now follow in Section 1.1.1, pay close attention to how the individuals:

- report the feelings associated with their behavioural experiences.
- explain the origins of these experiences and any associated behaviour.

These two types of information from the individual form what is termed a **personal narrative**. As this first chapter also describes the treatment of mental distress, you should consider whether medicine seems to you to be the appropriate treatment in each case, or whether some other form of treatment seems more appropriate.

1.1.1 How things can go wrong

John has obsessive–compulsive disorder (OCD), washing his hands excessively. He spends several hours a day scrubbing them in hot water and detergent, even though the skin is now damaged and causes pain. John has told his therapist, 'I have the repetitive and frightening intrusive thought that, unless I perform this ritual, something terrible will befall my family'. Having no idea why he started this behaviour five years ago, John has acknowledged 'an element of irrationality in my behaviour' but that does not permit him to

OCD comes in various forms, hand-washing being only one of the types of compulsion associated with the disorder. Other forms are described later.

stop. Medications have been tried but they make him sleepy and dizzy and produce a dry mouth.

The therapist is trying gradual exposure to the anxiety-evoking thoughts, during which John is urged to refrain from hand-washing. Whilst she is present, John is encouraged to reduce gradually the time he spends washing his hands and a record is kept of these times. John reported, 'particularly under stress, for example, at work, I have great trouble resisting my compulsion'. With the bathroom out of bounds to them for hours each day, his family cannot understand John's OCD. Sometimes, in desperation, they switch off the water supply. This triggers John's anger and a demand to switch it back on. He claims that, 'my family should understand me since there is a family history of OCD, though not in the form of hand-washing. This is clearly a genetic and brain disorder. That is why I am given medication'. (Figure 1.1)

Figure 1.1 How can a perfectly normal behaviour become excessive to the point of damaging part of the body?

Neha, a school teacher, has depression. She has recently moved from a close-knit community and extended family to a big city and she has had some painful life experiences, including the death of her parents and a traumatic divorce. Now on her own, she claims, 'these events caused my illness'. She is receiving counselling as well as antidepressant medication but has been off work for months.

Neha finds it difficult to get up in the morning and states, 'I can see no purpose in living'. Her mood is low, her thoughts being dominated by what she perceives as her failures in life, loss, inadequacy and death. Her self-esteem has plummeted to a low level. The therapist is trying to change Neha's patterns of negative thinking by getting her to monitor and challenge the accuracy of her own silent speech – 'are you really a failure at everything?' Neha's family telephone to appeal to her regularly with 'pull yourself together', advice that sends her into tears and elicits the reply that she feels totally alone and helpless. In addition, Neha is experiencing aches and pains in her body, which were never there before. She feels flu-like symptoms. (Figure 1.2)

Figure 1.2 What is it like to experience depression?

Jim has had a near-fatal heart attack and has been ordered by his doctor to take life easier. Although he smoked and ate the wrong foods, everyone but Jim suspects that his style of 'workaholism' played a role in the disorder. He was a commodities trader and lived only to make money. No matter what the damage and in the face of humiliating failures, Jim needed always to try to be at the top of the pecking order. Even when passing through an acrimonious divorce, he never acknowledged any psychological disturbance. He claims, 'my heart attack was nothing to do with my behaviour'. However, Jim admits that, 'I find it impossible to delegate' and he shows hostility when he can't get his own way. It was during an outburst of anger that Jim suddenly felt, in his words, 'as if a red-hot iron was being driven into my chest' – his first heart attack. He has been told to take time off work, and to monitor and challenge his hostile thoughts – which he does with much reluctance.

With similar reluctance, Jim has agreed to try meditation as a means of relaxation. (Figure 1.3)

Figure 1.3 How might such an environment be damaging to health?

Angie is showing signs of mental disturbance, taking the form of auditory hallucinations ('hearing voices'). At first, she tried to ignore the strange mental events and no one seemed to notice that anything was wrong. Then the intense fear became insufferable and she sought help. Now 19 years old, since the age of 12 she has smoked a form of potent cannabis, termed 'skunk'. Her parents are divided on what to think. Angie's father believes her account of the voices and blames the drug. However, her mother thinks that Angie is fabricating a 'good story', claiming that she is a malingerer. As part of her personal narrative, Angie states, 'my troubles arise from having bad parents', and adds, 'they are why I started smoking cannabis in the first place'. (Figure 1.4)

Mary, a survivor of child abuse, has never been happy and is now addicted to heroin. She suggests, 'without the history of abuse, I would never be in this mess'. Mary lives in a slum tenement and now also has an abusive partner. She pleads, 'drugs are a crutch that keep me going'. Mary acknowledges that, in the long term, she would be better off without the heroin but short-term considerations of getting through each day dominate. She says that she feels 'relatively normal' only when taking the drug. Mary has tried coming off heroin but, each time, a new source of stress appears in her life and she turns to this 'chemical crutch' to lift her mood. A major source of stress was unemployment. She has used legally prescribed substitute drugs but they don't have the same effect. Mary experiences intense wanting of heroin (termed 'craving').

Figure 1.4 Why might a young person turn to cannabis as a solution to their problems and what effect could the drug have?

Craving can be set off by bad events in her life or by being in the presence of reminders of drug-taking such as the sight of a syringe or the other addicts she knows. She experiences withdrawal symptoms including sweating and shaking and these can also be triggered by being in a drug-related environment. Mary's family have turned their back on her, claiming that she is just weak-willed. (Figure 1.5)

Mark is suffering from a serious deterioration in his memory. Now aged 65, he was a journalist and keen sportsman. Mark is entirely dependent upon his

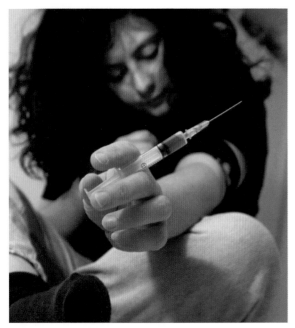

Figure 1.5 What sort of dilemma underlies such behaviour and how can we gain insight into it?

carers. Medication can only slow the decline. His wife is devoted to giving him round-the-clock care. Mark still has insight into the memory loss and, in his mind, he notes his lapses: 'I know my memory is not what it was but I can't explain why'. Unlike a few years ago, he cannot now remember where his wife has parked their car and leaves the gas switched on. Everyone is sympathetic to Mark and his family, acknowledging that little can be done to halt the decline.

In each of these cases, there is deterioration in the quality of life, compared to either before the condition or how the individuals would like things to be. None of them is happy with his or her condition. What might be used as a measure of mental ill-health in these cases? Consider the following.

Subjective and objective reports

In understanding mental ill-health, the **subjective report** of the individual, as part of the personal narrative, provides invaluable insight. The term 'subjective' refers to the perspective of the person reporting on the contents of his or her conscious mind. This is inaccessible to everyone else, except by listening to these reports.

- In the accounts, where does subjective evidence bear witness to mental distress?

  □ John reports obsessive thoughts that occupy his conscious mind. He wants to stop his hand-washing, which causes distress. However, after just a short time away from the bathroom, he is overcome with dread that something awful will happen. Neha expresses her distress in terms of a low mood and dark thoughts. Although denying that anything within his mind or behaviour was responsible for the heart attack, Jim admits to feeling extreme hostility. Angie is frightened by the abnormal events that invade her mind. Mary reports low mood when she is not on drugs. A 'part of her' would love to be off drugs but she is frightened to face life without them. Mark is aware of his loss of memory.

Such subjective reports can be viewed alongside **objective measures** of ill-health, such as abnormalities in brain activity, heart rate, behaviour or levels of chemicals in the blood. An objective measure is one that can be observed and literally measured by another individual. In practice, it might sometimes be hard to obtain objective measures but in principle they are available.

- In the cases described, what are some objective measures of things not being right?

  □ John's hand-washing can be measured (e.g. length of time per day) and the effects on his skin documented. For Jim, there is observable disturbance to his heart. Mary's addiction can be indexed in terms of the frequency of injections and the quantity of drug taken. Mark's failing memory can be observed in terms of such things as forgetting to switch off the gas.

Evidence of Neha's distress is mainly in terms of her subjective reports, although her inability to rise in the morning is an objective measure. A principal task of psychology is to try to relate subjective and objective evidence in order to obtain as comprehensive a profile as is possible.

A look at such cases raises a number of further issues and exemplifies some phenomena associated with mental ill-health and how psychologists explain it, as follows (Box 1.1).

Box 1.1 Research Methods: Types of research

SDK228 is concerned with describing *how* things are in mental health. It aims to provide insights into the experience of mental health disorders: in other words, what it *feels* like to be in these states. In addition, scientists try to understand *why* people are the way that they are. Why do some people become depressed or why do others brim with happiness? What is it about the environment and genetics that tends to make some people depressed? To get answers, research is conducted on individuals or populations of participants. This research can be classified into two types, termed **quantitative** and **qualitative**.

Quantitative research is where researchers attempt literally to attribute numbers or 'quantities' to what they are studying. So, suppose that they are studying excessive and damaging ('obsessive') hand-washing and wish to measure the effect of a new medicine designed to treat this. They need some measure of how much hand-washing participants were performing prior to taking the new medicine and after taking it. So, records might be made of the length of time a person spends hand-washing each day before and after taking the medicine. This is *objective* research based upon observable and measurable phenomena. In this case, an experiment is performed in which the variables are controlled by the researcher: for example, the amount of medicine prescribed and exactly who receives the medicine. Other types of quantitative research may depend on results of surveys or questionnaires, where people answer questions on their symptoms or feelings. Careful design of questions can yield responses that can be analysed numerically. Data can also be obtained from observations of different groups of people: for example, it might be desirable to compare the incidence of obsessive hand-washing among men and women. Obtaining quantifiable data from experiments or observations in order to gain insights into mental health is the principal concern of SDK228.

By contrast, qualitative research emphasises the experiences and feelings of the participants. It can be used alongside quantitative research in order to obtain a more complete picture of the phenomenon under study. To return to the example of obsessive hand-washing, putting numbers onto the behaviour by measuring the hours spent washing yields objective evidence. However, some would argue that this misses an important aspect of the phenomenon: what it feels like to be plagued with intrusive thoughts of contamination. Only the person concerned could describe what it feels like and the content of those thoughts. This is *subjective* evidence and has a *quality* to it.

A commonly used qualitative method is an interview which allows the researcher to explore an issue with an individual. Interviews can be informal or structured around a set of questions. Qualitative evidence can also be obtained from observation of groups or individuals, small group discussions and focus groups. Written qualitative evidence from participants can be provided in questionnaires, open letters or diary entries. These techniques provide detailed information about how a phenomenon feels to an individual and how these feelings vary from person to person.

There are clear benefits of both types of research. Quantitative research allows the researcher to measure factors accurately and to analyse relationships between events. Experiments can be performed to verify or refute an observation or a hypothesis. Qualitative research, on the other hand, allows a more in-depth analysis of individual experiences and the recording of phenomena that cannot easily be quantified.

An element of irrationality and ambivalence

In some cases, people admit to some irrationality in their behaviour.

■ Give two examples of this from the cases described above.

☐ John acknowledges that his behaviour is excessive. He admits that it is unlikely that tragedy could be prevented by his hand-washing but finds such reasoning ineffective in the face of the compulsion. Mary acknowledges that, in the long term, she is doing harm. A 'bit of her' wants to come off heroin but short-term considerations win each time.

The ambivalence of John and Mary is a feature of both OCD and addiction. It is as if two parts of the mind are in competition to gain control of behaviour.

The big picture

SDK228 takes a broad perspective on understanding mental health and ill-health, drawing on various sources of evidence from biology, psychology and the social world. This section introduces this broad perspective, starting with biology.

John, Neha and Mark are taking prescribed medication. Mary is performing 'self-medication' and has tried a prescribed drug as a substitute for heroin. Medications of the types considered here, whether legal or illegal, are chemicals that have effects upon the brain. This will be explored throughout SDK228. As the brain, the target of such drugs, is part of the physical body, it is clear then that the study of *biology* plays a key role in understanding mental distress and its treatment.

In addition to medication, John is receiving a form of therapy that directly targets behaviour. In Neha's case, the chemical medication is accompanied by a form of 'talking therapy' which targets her thinking. Obviously, *psychology* will play a crucial role in understanding mental distress. John and Neha exemplify that use of a chemical can be compatible with using non-chemical forms of intervention.

Jim has also been asked to challenge 'negative thoughts'. This prescription, together with that of meditation, points to the therapist's belief that a successful change in his *mental* state would have beneficial influences throughout his *body*.

Neha's and Mary's *social* circumstances are such that they would be expected to play a role in understanding the distress they are experiencing. Any solution might necessitate changing these circumstances for the better.

Most people might well unambiguously characterise all of the disorders described as *abnormalities* of the mind and behaviour.

Activity 1.1 What does 'abnormality' mean?

(LO 1.1) Allow 5 minutes

Stop and think about the word 'abnormality' and what it means. Write a short paragraph on what you understand by the term.

Jim has never complained about his behaviour or mental state, though doubtless his subordinates have done so behind his back. Rather, the disorder, as Jim experienced and interpreted it, was one of his heart and, in his view, it is here that attention needed to be focused. However, contrary to Jim's beliefs, it is known that psychological events arising within the mind (e.g. hostility) are associated with powerful influences in various regions of the body (Williams, 1989). Chapter 2 describes how mental events are able to exert such influences.

Neha reports mysterious aches and pains as well as flu-like symptoms. This raises the possibility that her disturbed mental state has something to do with the emergence of such apparent bodily symptoms. If no such symptoms can be found in the body, the psychological events are sometimes described as **somatisation** (Dimsdale and Creed, 2009). The word 'soma' means body and the term 'somatisation' refers to psychological events that take the form of feeling pain and discomfort in regions of the body.

Finding causes

A major task in studying when things go wrong is to establish 'what causes the disorder'. The personal narrative needs to be considered as one possible source of insight but should be placed alongside objective evidence.

Jim's hostile behaviour was thought by his doctor and everyone around him to be a powerful factor in his heart attack, but so were his eating habits and smoking. Angie's parents blamed her smoking of cannabis, but she blamed their behaviour ('the social context'). Her mental disturbance could be the result of a combination of both factors. The hallucinations might have led her to taking cannabis as self-medication. So, how do we find the 'real cause' of the distress described? Chapter 4 of this book will examine this. Mary cites unemployment as having a destructive effect and indeed research evidence confirms the association between unemployment and poor mental health (Paul et al., 2009).

Sympathy and understanding

Explaining something in biological terms seems to link with the issue of sympathy. Everyone is sympathetic to Mark, presumably based on the assumption that the condition is a brain disorder and is beyond his control. Neha's family blame her for not 'pulling herself together'. John's family cannot understand why he acts as he does. Mary's family have long ceased to take any responsibility for her and have no sympathy. Throughout SDK228, you will come to critically question social attitudes taken towards mental ill-health.

Equally insightful to the study of mental health are examples of people living lives that we might characterise as psychologically healthy, discussed next.

1.1.2 Exemplifying mental well-being

If a friend said, 'I have an appointment with a psychologist', you would probably assume that something is wrong. As with medicine in general, the implicit assumption in psychology has been one of 'putting right what is wrong'. However, in the last few years, a new movement has emerged, termed **positive psychology** (described more fully in Book 2). Rather than the traditional focus on 'things going wrong', positive psychology focuses on healthy mental life and how it can be achieved.

Adherents of positive psychology employ the concept of **subjective well-being** (SWB) (Diener, 2000). People are said to experience SWB when they (p. 34):

> ... feel many pleasant and few unpleasant emotions, when they are engaged in interesting activities, when they experience many pleasures and few pains, and when they are satisfied with their lives.

In the case of well-being, the subjective index is of primary importance. Attempts to measure SWB rely on personal reports given by individuals. The following three cases illustrate features of life that are, according to positive psychology, associated with a relatively high SWB.

Ho, a teacher, married and with children, is in good health. He is active in sports and charity work. His life, which he describes as 'having purpose' and 'being meaningful', is characterised by balance between work and leisure. Ho is absorbed in his work and feels that he contributes to the well-being of the community. His job places heavy demands on him but he can meet these. Although he is seeking promotion, whether or not he gets it is 'no big deal'. Ho is popular with his colleagues and values friendship above the acquisition of material possessions. (Figure 1.6)

Claudia, a farmer, has stress in her life and yet she manages to weather the storms and describes herself as coping with life. Change has come only gradually to her village and Claudia knows her neighbours well. The community thrives on the basis of trust and mutual support: no one is rich but neither does anyone 'go without'. People experience 'belonging' to the community. Claudia has few material possessions and attributes her resilience mainly to her stable marriage and being part of an extended family. The church provides support when times are hard. Claudia is rarely ill and enjoys her job. (Figure 1.7)

Henry, a gardener, is unable to divide work and pleasure. A country-lover, who has a sense of wonder in nature, he derives much pleasure from taking long walks. He has three dogs and attributes a calming influence to them. Henry is on good terms with his neighbours and feels part of a cohesive social network. He puts his good health down to 'family influence' – 'I got good genes from my parents. Never any melancholy in their lives'. If ever he feels stressed, Henry takes exercise in the form of running across country with his dogs and visiting a distant and now house-bound farmer. He claims that the exertion of muscular effort gets him on a 'high'.

Figure 1.6 How can a person's goals in life contribute to psychological well-being?

Each of these people exemplifies something about good psychological health, as follows:

Social cohesiveness

Each person forms part of a cohesive social network, experiences 'belonging' and shows altruism towards others. Belonging and altruism are good for mental health (Post, 2007).

Lack of negative emotion

Each of the three people shows an absence of competitiveness and hostility. They have harmony and contentment with their lot in life.

Coping

There is not necessarily a complete lack of day-to-day potential triggers to stress in their lives. Rather, they have coping strategies for dealing with the stresses that arise from time to time. Being part of a family and wider community buffers them against the harmful effects of stress (Baumeister and Leary, 1995).

General physical health

People having a healthy psychological life tend also to show good physical health (Marks and Shah, 2005), which points to the intimate link between mind and body. The word to note is 'tend' – there is no guarantee of an

Figure 1.7 What is the role of social context in psychological well-being and good health?

illness-free existence but there are strong associations between psychological health and general health.

Genetics

Henry mentions the possibility that genetics plays a role in his well-being. This raises the issue of whether differences in genes between people can play a role in differences in their mental states.

Absence of materialist values

None of the three emphasises materialist values as having importance in their lives, which exemplifies a general tendency: those who pursue materialist aims tend to have a lower well-being than those whose aims are more socially cohesive (Kasser, 2002). Of course, below a certain level of income, people do experience low levels of well-being but, above such a limit, increasing wealth does not lead to increased well-being.

Purpose

The three have a purpose in their existence; they describe themselves as being 'engaged in life'. Ho's work involves positive interaction with others and goals that can realistically be achieved. All three enjoy their work, an important factor in well-being (Marks and Shah, 2005).

■ In regard to having a purpose in life, how might you compare and contrast Ho (above) and Jim (Section 1.1.1)?

☐ In a sense, both have a purpose to which they strive. However, whereas Ho's is based upon positive interactions with his fellow humans, Jim's is based on struggle and hostility. Ho's goal can realistically be achieved, whereas Jim's appears to be elusive.

Having given some examples of mental health and ill-health, the chapter now turns to the issue of explaining how these phenomena arise.

1.2 The nature of explanations of mental health and ill-health

1.2.1 Introduction

Humans do not just observe the behaviour of themselves and others but they try to explain it, both as part of a *personal narrative* concerning events in their lives and as part of professional research and intervention. Implicit in the cases introduced in Section 1.1 is the notion of *cause*. It is a working assumption that mental health and disorder do not just arise spontaneously but something happens to cause them to occur. As you will see, the kinds of treatment that are devised often mirror the suggested causes of the disorders.

The joint assumption that mental events are caused to occur and these causes can sometimes be found has given much insight. However, in some cases, the causes remain elusive. For example, it might prove difficult to establish what made John start compulsive hand-washing, but he speculates that something has gone wrong with his brain. Life events, such as bereavement and divorce, were suggested as the cause of Neha's depression, whereas hostility seemed to be the trigger to Jim's heart attack. On a more cheerful note, Claudia refers to community support, whereas Ho describes having purposes in life. This section will look at some issues raised by attempts to explain mental health and ill-health, starting with the earliest.

1.2.2 Accounts in early history

Historically, attempts to explain mental distress appealed either to supernatural forces or to events in the body or the external environment. For example, epilepsy was seen as an affliction sent by the Gods. In terms of supernatural events, mental disease has frequently been seen as an expression of the taking over of the body by some demonic influence. Witches were attributed a role in commanding the demons to do their dirty work. Not surprisingly, treatments would often appeal to supernatural interventions, as in exorcism, a technique that survives even to the present.

By contrast, other explanations have appealed to abnormality arising in the body. Within this tradition, accounts can be traced back to early Arab writers and to ancient Greece, particularly to the writing of Hippocrates (460 BC– 377 BC). According to Hippocrates, the body contains four different types of fluids, termed 'humours'. Healthy individuals have a balance between these fluids, whereas illness is associated with an excess of one type.

Changes can be observed over time in what is, or is not, classed as an illness. Imagine going to your doctor complaining of 'lovesickness'. You might like to try this but don't be disappointed if you get a look of amazement and the answer: 'I have no idea what to prescribe'. The notion of seeking medical help for this condition will surely seem amusing these days, but for much of recorded human history it would not have been considered in the least unusual. For example, records are very good from 16th century England. Dawson (2008, p. 2) writes:

> ... intense unfulfilled erotic desire is classified as a species of melancholy, with mental and physiological etiologies and cures ... authors held erotic obsession to be a real and virulent disease.

The term 'etiology' or 'aetiology' refers to the origins or causes of a disease, whereas 'physiology' refers to the functioning of the body, so 'physiological etiologies' here refers to causes within the body (see Chapter 4).

So 'virulent' indeed was the disease believed to be that, if caught in a sufficiently large dose and without cure, it was assumed to be ultimately lethal. As far as the basis of the 'virulent disease' was concerned, writers attributed it to (Dawson, 2008, p. 2):

> ... a burning in the blood and liver, as a humoral imbalance, as an image fixed in the mind, or as the product of seed or sperm.

Correspondingly, one possible cure prescribed was the removal of an amount of blood.

You could be forgiven for giggling over these early accounts, but note one important feature that is consistent with present-day understanding: the attempt to integrate psychological factors within the mind and biological factors in the body. Abnormalities in the body were seen to be triggers to mental distress.

Moving on to nearer the present time, the 19th century saw the broad acceptance that there is a link between features of the mind and *regions of the brain*. For example, evidence showed that damage to parts of the brain was associated with particular disturbances to mind and behaviour. So, logically, the brain was seen as a target for interventions in the case of mental disorder. Psychologically distressed people have had parts of their brains removed or powerful electric currents passed through their brains as treatments. The rationale was that such interventions would alter the workings of the brain in some way and thereby alter the state of the mind.

Subjective evidence of mental suffering has not been the only criterion for making interventions. Of course, being judged as a potential danger to oneself or others is another consideration. Also moral issues and uncritical use of the notion of 'abnormality' have played a role. For example, until the 1970s, homosexuality was classed as a mental disorder within the psychiatric profession, something to be corrected by therapy. Subsequently homosexuality became more accepted and surely these days few would wish to classify gay people as candidates for treatment. So, some relativity exists in what is classified as a mental illness or disorder but there remains a core notion of human psychological suffering that surely cuts across time periods.

Lay accounts reveal assumptions about 'what causes what' in mind and behaviour. Recall that Mary's family had deserted her on the grounds that she was simply 'weak-willed'. Earlier generations might have described an addict like Mary as 'morally weak'.

Activity 1.2 Language with powerful implications
(LOs 1.1 and 1.3) Allow 10 minutes

More recently, there has been a tendency to describe people like Mary as 'having a disease'. Do you think that this is a useful way of viewing Mary's drug-related behaviour? Is it an advance over the description 'weak-willed'? How do the cases of Neha and John relate to these questions? Make short notes on some of the implications of the words chosen.

1.2.3 More recent ways of explaining mental health and ill-health

The biomedical model

Until quite recent years, there was a popular view of disease that was summarised by the expression **biomedical model** (see Engel, 1977). This suggested that disease is, *by definition*, associated with identifiable disturbances to the body and can be defined in terms of such disturbance. A cure would consist in correcting the disturbance. So, by this criterion, cancer is clearly a disease, as is an artery blocked by fatty substances. An infection by a virus is a disease, since the virus represents an invasion of something harmful to the body.

According to a biomedical model, only diseases defined in this way are the business of the medical profession. Where there is no such identifiable disturbance, then there might well be distress but this is not a medical matter. Rather, it is the concern of, amongst others, psychologists, counsellors, priests, family members or social workers. By this criterion, if a form of mental distress has as its cause a measurable basis in a bodily disturbance, then it is a disease for which medicine is the obvious treatment. If it does not have such a basis, it should not be defined or treated as a disease.

Some non-medical professionals, concerned with alleviating mental distress, were happy to subscribe to the biomedical model. Thereby, they defined their own domain of expertise and responsibility in terms of psychological distress that did not fit the criteria of disease. In this way, such professionals arrived at a clear dichotomy between what *is or is not* a disease, based upon biological criteria.

There are numerous problems with the biomedical model. Even if there is a disturbance somewhere in the body, it is not usually this as such that will cause an individual to present for treatment (Engel, 1977). Rather, most often, they will present because of some form of pain, discomfort or distress as *subjectively experienced*. There will be a cultural and social dimension in how such expression of distress is made and help sought. Biology alone cannot give the full picture.

Some suggested that the biomedical model has a universal application to all forms of distress, whether or not there is an identifiable disorder in the body. Hence, no matter what the distress, presumably a biological intervention in the form of medicine would be appropriate.

Activity 1.3 Value of the biomedical model

(LO 1.1) Allow 20 minutes

Stop and reflect on this issue. Do you think that the biomedical model is appropriate for understanding the people introduced in Section 1.1.1?

At this point you should stop to consider what a model actually is. A model is a bit like a theory in that it is only an idea of how things are, or how things work. It is a hypothesised representation. The important thing to remember is that unless there is evidence to support a model being correct it is essentially just someone's idea. Models should be testable in that they should enable predictions to be made which can be supported, or refuted, by study evidence. As an example, consider the famous historical myth of Magellan and the flat Earth. The story (not true but it was taught in schools until fairly recently!) goes that the model of the Earth that had prevailed until the time of Magellan was that the Earth was flat. Thus if a ship kept sailing in one direction it would eventually reach the edge and be at risk of falling off. This latter part is a prediction that the model made which could be tested. According to the story, Magellan refuted the flat Earth model when he sailed around the world and didn't fall off but instead headed out west and came back from the east, thus showing that the Earth was round. Granted this is a myth rather than a real example, but it illustrates rather nicely that you should never take a model at face value and consider it as hard evidence of the way things are. You will discover more about using models in detail in Book 3, Chapter 3.

The biopsychosocial model

The term 'biopsychosocial perspective' is also used here.

You might feel that the cases described in Section 1.1 suggest that a full understanding of mental distress, as well as mental health, involves a study of the biology of the body (usually with an emphasis upon the brain), individual psychology and social circumstances. This perspective is summarised by the expression **biopsychosocial model** (Engel, 1977) and it rejects the neat dichotomies of the biomedical model. According to this model, disease, defined *simply* in terms of biology, is not a useful way of approaching distress and well-being.

A central assumption behind the biopsychosocial model is that, not only do the three factors, biological, psychological and social, play a role in *any* form of psychological distress or well-being, but also that there is *interdependence* between them (Figure 1.8). For example, changing an individual's social circumstances can change his or her psychology and changing an individual's psychology can change their social interactions. Changing a person's psychological state will change the activity of their brain. In these terms, biology is not an absolute defining criterion of when there is mental distress but neither is it irrelevant. Biological abnormality can contribute to mental distress but it is only one contributory factor amongst three.

Figure 1.8 can serve as a framework for organising thinking and as a kind of check against making what some would regard as simplistic assumptions regarding mental health and ill-health. In terms of this approach, it serves as a caution against a dichotomy of the kind that a mental disorder could be 'purely biological' or 'purely psychological'. Similarly, it cautions against a dichotomy that the effects of a treatment might be *either* biological *or* psychological as exclusive categories.

In health or ill-health, biological *and* psychological contributions will always be present. In one sense, in the very rare cases of, for example, a person living alone on a desert island or a hermit in a cave, there will not be a social factor present. However, such a person will still have had a history of earlier social interactions which will have left their mark. So, according to a biopsychosocial model, the relevant question is not which factor, 'bio', 'psycho' or 'social', is the most important, since they are totally interdependent. Rather, Figure 1.8 draws attention to the fact that changes in all three factors can arise from biological, psychological or social changes. At whichever of the three boxes the change arises, there will be consequences at the other two boxes.

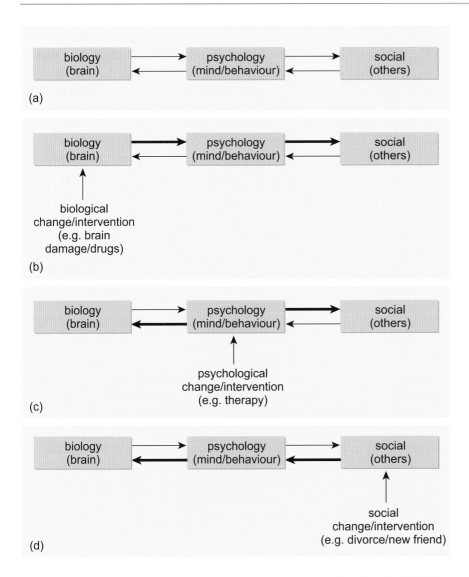

Figure 1.8 (a) The biopsychosocial model, demonstrating interdependence between factors. (b) Changes/interventions in the biology of the brain (e.g. brain damage or drugs) have effects on psychology and thereby can alter social context. (c) Psychological changes/interventions (e.g. a form of therapy) will alter the brain and can change social context. (d) A social change/intervention (e.g. a new friend) will alter psychology, and thereby have effects on the biology of the brain.

Take, for example, a tumour which disturbs the levels of certain hormones in the body. Suppose that these hormones affect the brain and hence their changed levels form an input as shown in Figure 1.8b. Changing the activity of the brain changes the person's psychology (e.g. to trigger depression), with effects on their social world. Consider now that a person receives some kind of counselling, therapy or pastoral care such that their psychological condition changes. Figure 1.8c shows implications for their social world and their biology. The link to the social world is rather obvious, as in, for example, becoming more outgoing socially. The link to biology is not so obvious but, throughout Book 1, justification will be given for the assumption that changing 'psychology' inevitably alters the 'biology' of the brain. Finally,

Hormones are introduced in Chapter 2. For the moment, you can simply regard them as chemicals that have various effects throughout the body.

Figure 1.8d shows a social change, such as divorce or marriage or finding a new job. This has obvious implications for a person's psychology, which simultaneously affects the brain. A change does not necessarily occur in only one of the three factors at any one time. Consider, for example, Mary's drug-taking. Drugs are chemicals, which act at the biological level. However, Mary is not simply a passive recipient of such chemicals. Rather, she will have certain expectations about their effects, as learned through her history of drug-taking and cultural transmission of information from her social contacts with other drug-users. This will constitute an input to the 'psychology' box in parallel with that to the 'biology' box. Mary's expectation about the effect of a given intervention is an example of the **placebo effect** (see Box 1.2).

Box 1.2 Research Methods: The role of the placebo

Research has shown that part of the efficacy of mood-altering drugs is due to expectations about their effect – an example of the placebo effect (Reinarman and Levine, 1997). Similarly, a part of the efficacy of the pain-reducing drug morphine is due to such expectations about its effect (Beecher, 1955). The placebo effect means that when a drug company wishes to introduce a new product, its effect must be checked 'against a placebo' (Stewart-Williams and Podd, 2004). That is to say, two groups of participants would be treated identically in terms of receiving a substance but only one group would receive the new drug. The other group would receive a chemically inert substance. Neither group would know what they were receiving. Placebo trials often find that the group taking the placebo shows some improvement (e.g. in mood) compared to taking nothing at all. For the new drug to receive a licence for sale, a beneficial effect 'above that of placebo' would need to be demonstrated.

The chapter now turns to reconsider the cases in Section 1.1, in the light of a biopsychosocial perspective.

Brain events

Everyone around him believes that Mark's loss of memory is the result of disturbed processes within his brain. John believes that an abnormality in his brain is at the basis of his OCD. The fact that chemicals are prescribed in the cases of John, Neha and Mary is testimony to the implicit assumptions that (a) these chemicals act on the brain and (b) when they work, it is by changing the brain (Figure 1.8b). However, in addition to the specific role of the drug, a placebo effect must also be considered to play a possible role.

Mental events

Ho has goals in life, ones that he can consciously articulate. Jim's mind was occupied with hostile thoughts and one prescription was for him to challenge this thinking. Although the prime causes of Neha's mental distress appeared to be external to her, the therapist feels that her repetitive negative thought patterns could form the target of intervention. The term **cognition** is employed to describe mental processes, for example of this kind. An intervention that acts at the level of thoughts is said to be **cognitive**. From a biopsychosocial perspective, how do brain events and mental events relate to each other?

Relating mental events and brain events

People in mental distress will usually describe their experiences in terms of events within their conscious minds: for example, their pains, fears and aspirations. Therapists and researchers can use these subjective reports and try to understand them. In addition, they might have objective evidence – on events in the person's brain, for example.

The following assumption forms a foundation of biological psychology and is compatible with Figure 1.8 (the evidence for it will be described throughout SDK228):

> Brain events and mental events are intimately related, such that, for each mental event, there is a corresponding brain event.

SDK228 is based upon the acceptance of this principle.

A caution needs to be added at this point: this is merely a working assumption ('guiding principle') that seems to make sense of brain and mind. It is broadly implicit within research and therapy. Considerable evidence points to its validity (discussed in Chapter 2). Without doubt, insight can be gained and understanding reinforced by trying to relate events in the mind to those in the brain. However, the basic assumption is, so far, lacking conclusive proof as an all-pervasive truth, since it is impossible to prove that every mental event always has a correlate in an event in the brain.

So, consider, for example, Neha's depression. This might be described in subjective terms of her mental suffering, feeling of despair and negative thinking. From Neha's perspective, she, indeed *she alone*, has access to these events. As outsiders, other people only know of their existence if Neha chooses to tell them, though they might speculate accurately based upon her appearance and behaviour.

Biologically orientated psychologists assume that, for these events in Neha's mind, there are corresponding events happening in her brain. For example, at exactly the same time as Neha's subjectively experienced mood changes, so parallel changes occur in her brain. Suppose Neha recovers from depression. No longer is she assailed by thoughts of failure and death. The assumption is that exactly corresponding to this change in mental events in Neha's conscious mind are particular changes in her brain. This is true no matter what form of therapy was employed, if any at all.

Based on this assumption, the term 'brain–mind' can be used to refer to the combination of brain and mind, with both components changing in parallel.

■ Try applying the brain–mind assumption just developed to what happens in Mary's drug-taking.

☐ In the absence of the drug, Mary's mental state is one of negative emotion, which corresponds to a particular pattern of brain activity. The drug locks onto Mary's brain, which changes its pattern of activity. Corresponding to this change in brain activity, Mary's consciously felt mood improves.

An account of Mark's loss of memory would be along the following lines. The basis of dementia is that, for reasons that are not entirely clear, parts of the brain become damaged. This damage alters the mind in a way that corresponds to the loss of conscious access to memories. In Mark's case, it is interesting to speculate as to whether the biological type of explanation ('biomedical model') is all that is needed, or whether a biopsychosocial perspective is also needed even here (this perspective is described in Book 4).

Social context

Stress arising at work or in domestic relationships exacerbates John's OCD and Mary's drug-taking. Claudia attributes her well-being to her community. Neha's depression is attributed to events happening in her social world – the death of her parents and divorce (Figure 1.8d). Neha's case can be used to illustrate the general principle.

In one sense, from Neha's perspective, the loss of her parents and husband happened in the social world 'out there'. However, the events 'out there' were observed by Neha and interpreted by her brain–mind, so they were simultaneously 'out there' and represented inside her brain–mind. Neha attributed *meaning* to these external events (part of a personal narrative), in terms of what their significance was for her. For one person, a partner walking out would be felt as the end of the world, whereas for another, it might be greeted with indifference or even relief. Similarly, what might be a highly stressful work environment for one person, to another might be seen as simply a welcome challenge. So:

> For the purpose of understanding their role in mental health and ill-health, such social events need to be described in terms of their representation and meaning within the minds of the individual concerned.

Inheritance

John argues that there is a family history of OCD. Henry attributes his good psychological health to genes that he inherited from his parents. This could point to a role for inheritance in mental health and disorder through a genetic influence. (To represent this, the 'biology' box in Figure 1.8a would be different for different individuals because their genes are different.)

■   Can you think of an alternative to this exclusively genetic explanation?

☐   One generation imitating the behaviour of the previous, or perhaps both genetics and imitation are involved.

In Book 2, you will critically examine what role might be played by inheritance and how this is transmitted into mental health or ill-health.

At the point of fertilisation, genes from our mother and father come together. These genes play a role in determining the structure of all the regions of our body, including the brain. As a result of variations in genes, some brains might well have a different fine-grained form from that of others, in the sense that the individual is more likely later in life either to suffer from mental distress or conversely to experience well-being. Although life experience and circumstances contribute to subjective well-being, a component of it arises from inheritance (Diener, 2000). However, you will need to be on your guard against accepting over-simple assertions of the kind that well-being or OCD 'is in the genes' since this is to ignore the powerful role of the social environment.

1.2.4 Holism and reductionism

This section describes two related terms that are involved in explaining health and ill-health.

The term **holism** means taking into account the whole picture. A 'biopsychosocial perspective' is a form of holism. SDK228 will examine the three *interdependent factors*, biological, psychological and social, in devising explanations and possible interventions in mental health. From this perspective, all three factors are equally valid as objects of study.

The term **reductionism** refers to a process of trying to explain events, which stands in contrast to the notion of holism. There are slightly different but often overlapping ways of employing the term 'reductionism', each of which is a form of simplification. One way of using 'reductionism' is to describe the process of focusing on only one component of a complex whole. So, in explaining behaviour, a study of biology to the exclusion of psychology and social context would be said to be reductionist. Similarly, to explain psychology simply in terms of social context, whilst ignoring biology, would also exemplify reductionism in this sense.

Another shade of meaning of reductionism is in seeking explanations at a *smaller scale* (Figure 1.9). An example of this use of reductionism is searching for an explanation of mental, behavioural and social events in terms of activity of regions of the brain. To take such reductionism still further, activity of the different areas of the brain would then be explained in terms of the chemicals that make up the brain (neurochemicals), and the performance of these neurochemicals might then be explained in terms of their component parts. The biomedical model exemplifies reductionism in both of these senses. An exclusive focus upon social context to the exclusion of biology and psychology illustrates reductionism in only the first sense of the term.

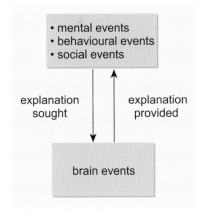

Figure 1.9 Reductionism.

You might consider that John is appealing to such a process of reductionism in explaining his OCD as something wrong with his brain. It rather depends upon whether he was placing an exclusive focus upon the brain, neglecting other factors. Reductionism can be a valuable process in that biological events clearly play a role in mental life and investigating them can yield vital insights. However, the danger comes in attributing an exclusive or privileged role to biological events. Might mental or social phenomena be equally valid as sources of insight or targets of intervention? For example, Mary's brain will surely be adversely affected by her social situation (Figure 1.8d). However, it might be considered insensitive to target her brain with drugs as the first-line solution to the problem (seeing her as 'brain disordered'), thereby downplaying potential social interventions. The study of the brain can be very seductive and has high status, such that some are led to see brain science as providing the *only* valid explanation and first-line target of intervention.

1.2.5 Comparing populations

The chapter has suggested that some causes of mental health and ill-health can be identified by looking at such things as life events (e.g. divorce, social isolation and unemployment). Given this approach, it is interesting for researchers to compare different societies in terms of their mental health and ill-health. If differences appear, the next logical step is to try to explain them in terms of events within the lives of the populations concerned.

Obsessive–compulsive disorder

Concerning OCD, Table 1.1 compares some of the most frequent themes of obsessions amongst four populations from different parts of the world (Okasha et al., 1994).

Table 1.1 Types of obsession in different parts of the world.

Location	Number	Contamination/ %	Aggressive/ %	Ordering/ %	Sexual/ %	Religious/ %
Egypt	90	60	41	53	47	60
India	82	46	29	27	10	11
England	45	38	23	11	9	0
Jerusalem	10	40	20	10	10	50

Note that the rows for the types of obsession do not add up to 100% since a number of people had multiple obsessions (e.g. a combination of a contamination and religious theme). A number of obsessions shown by the England group were outside the range of themes documented.

The nature of OCD appears to be very similar across cultures in the form of intrusive thoughts and compulsive behaviour that represents an attempt to neutralise the intrusion. Contamination is a dominant theme in all four samples (as for John in Section 1.1.1). However, religious themes engage 60% of the Egypt sample but 0% of the England sample. Cultural factors appear to 'write the script' for what the exact nature of the obsessional thought will be. The authors noted that religious rituals, designed to ward off blasphemous thoughts, feature large in Egyptian society where the term *weswas* refers to both the devil and obsessions.

Interestingly, even in people without OCD, there is a tendency for cleaning to be associated with cognitions of psychological impurity. For example, when someone recalls guilt-related events from their past, this tends to be followed by thoughts of cleaning and taking cleaning-related action (Zhong and Liljenqvist, 2006). All the great religions of the world have a notion of psychological cleansing from impurity.

Overall mental distress

Concerning overall mental distress, comparing 1977 and 1985, there appears to be an 8% increase in psychiatric illness in Britain (Lewis and Wilkinson, 1993). The authors were unable to explain this, though it is open to speculation. Comparing different countries would seem to be particularly risky, a daunting 'needle-in-a-haystack' challenge. The number of factors that might vary between populations is likely to be enormous. How can researchers be sure that the same criteria of ill-health and techniques of data collection are employed? They can't. However, such difficulties have not stood in the way of some fascinating speculation. As an example, consider the data presented by Pickett et al. (2009), shown in Figure 1.10. The 'prevalence of any mental illness/%' is based upon the mental health survey initiative of the World Health Organization.

It refers to the prevalence in the population of any serious mental illness. Income inequality was calculated as the ratio of the richest 20% of the population to the poorest 20%, based upon data from the United Nations. The data suggests that a large inequality of income within a country is associated with a high prevalence of mental illness. Conversely, even in countries where most people are relatively poor, there are lower rates of mental illness than among the poor in unequal societies. The explanation might well have something to do with higher social cohesion in countries with better mental health.

The term 'prevalence' is defined in Chapter 4.

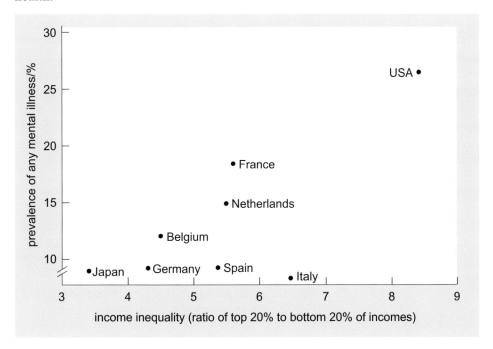

Figure 1.10 The relationship between income inequality and mental illness in eight countries.

Activity 1.4 The role of income inequality in mental illness

(LOs 1.1 and 1.2) Allow 10 minutes

As you look at Figure 1.10, think about what might explain this result.

The chapter now looks at some examples of interventions to treat distress and how these relate to the suggested causes of distress.

1.3   Relating the causes and treatments of distress

Our understanding of the causes of mental distress has links to the kinds of treatments employed. To exemplify this, the present section will reconsider some of the cases introduced in Section 1.1 and how insights into what has gone wrong relate to how to treat the individuals concerned.

1.3.1   Altering cognitions

Neha's case

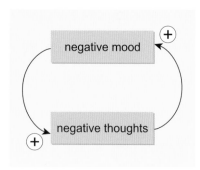

Figure 1.11   A cycle of causes.

Neha's mind was besieged by repetitive patterns of negative thinking, concerning events in her life. How could such patterns arise and how might they be treated? A particular mood has the effect of reviving memories that are in accordance with ('congruent with') that mood (Bower, 1981). Low moods help to revive bad memories, whereas good moods help to revive good memories. Neha's low mood would have made negative memories and interpretations of events particularly likely to occur. The low mood might then have locked into a 'vicious cycle' of interaction with her thought patterns (see Figure 1.11). That is to say, the low mood made negative thoughts more likely to arise in her conscious mind and, in turn, the negative thoughts exacerbated the low mood. A psychological form of therapy could consist in getting Neha to observe her patterns of thinking, to record them in a diary and challenge them. She would be asked to observe her behaviour and to document the things that she successfully achieved or that she had earlier achieved in her life. In effect, Neha would be asked to do an experiment to test the accuracy of her catastrophic thought pattern and to disprove the validity of some of the negative thoughts. With luck, this would undermine the negative thought pattern that, 'I am a failure at everything'. As her negative thinking changes, the depression should lift. This intervention is therefore targeted at a psychological level but, according to a biopsychosocial model, there would be a parallel change in brain events supporting this shift in cognition (Figure 1.8c).

Antidepressant medication could also have the effect of helping to break this vicious cycle of negative thinking. Suppose that antidepressant medication, in this case Prozac, was used successfully to treat Neha. Prozac is a type of chemical with known sites of action in the brain (explored further in Book 2). As the chemical acts on regions of Neha's brain, so the brain changes its activity and Neha's mental state would change correspondingly (Figure 1.8b).

John's case

As described in Section 1.1.1, a technique known as **response prevention** was being tried with John: getting him to live with the anxiety caused by his obsessive thoughts and not to wash his hands. The basis of this is the assumption that anxiety will decline and hence there will not be the trigger to hand-washing.

Why should anxiety decline? Current thinking is as follows (Salkovskis, 1999). At 'one level' in John's mind, he believes that hand-washing is protecting his family from catastrophe. Indeed, this strategy might appear to work, since the family has not suffered any catastrophe. So long as John washes his hands and nothing terrible happens to the family, John's belief is confirmed. Because these thoughts were so anxiety-evoking, John never got to do the experiment that would disprove this hypothesis. If the therapist can persuade John to refrain from washing for long enough, this might re-tune John's cognition from [washing] → [no catastrophe] to [either washing or no washing] → [no catastrophe].

This section has looked at the targeting of cognitions, though changes in behaviour are closely associated with any changed cognitions. The next section looks at techniques that target behaviour directly, and reciprocally it would be expected that any changes in behaviour are accompanied by underlying changes in cognition.

1.3.2 Conditioning

This section describes two forms of learning (termed 'conditioning'), which are relevant to how behaviour arises and how undesired behaviour such as OCD can be treated.

Classical conditioning

Mary reported that drug urges and some withdrawal effects were triggered by contexts associated in the past with drug-taking, such as the sight of a syringe or seeing certain friends. This suggests what is termed **classical conditioning** (Siegel, 2005). Classical conditioning was first demonstrated experimentally by Pavlov. Figure 1.12 illustrates this.

A dog normally salivates to the presence of meat in its mouth. It does not normally salivate to the sound of a metronome (Figure 1.12a), so the sound is termed a 'neutral stimulus'. In Pavlov's experiment, on a number of occasions, immediately prior to giving meat, a sound was made (Figure 1.12b). After a time, the dog came to salivate to the sound, even if it was not followed by meat (Figure 1.12c). In other words, the sound acquired a new capacity: to activate salivation, by virtue of its earlier pairing with the presentation of meat. The power of the sound is said to be *conditional* upon such pairing. It has no 'unconditional' power to trigger salivation. This explains the origin of the term 'conditioning'. The adjective 'classical' is to credit Pavlov with being the first to demonstrate conditioning scientifically (another type of conditioning is described next). The sound of the metronome is said to be a **conditional stimulus**. Its efficacy is 'conditional upon' its pairing with the meat.

Note that the dog had no control over the sequence of outside events, the timing of the sound and the meat. These were entirely in Pavlov's hands. The significance of this will become apparent in a moment when another form of conditioning is described.

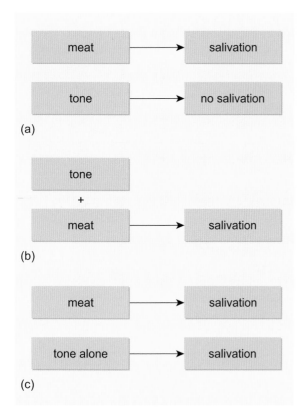

Figure 1.12 Classical conditioning.

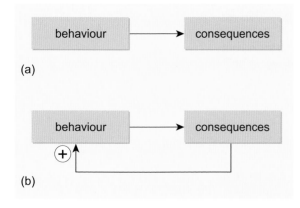

Figure 1.13 Behaviour and one of its possible consequences. (a) General case. (b) Case where reinforcement occurs.

To relate this to Mary's case, drug-related apparatus, locations and friends have been associated in the past with withdrawal symptoms and craving. When they are present, something of Mary's drug urges and withdrawal symptoms reappear. There are two possible ways to treat Mary that are suggested by these considerations. First, would be to try to help her to move to an environment not associated with drug-taking. Second, could be to attempt controlled exposure to drug-related stimuli, but in the absence of taking the drug. A therapist might repeatedly expose Mary to the sight of the heroin and a syringe but urge her to refrain from injection. This is termed applying **extinction conditions**. With luck, in time the urges might decline, a phenomenon termed **extinction**.

Instrumental conditioning

Another form of conditioning is termed **instrumental conditioning**. To understand how a particular behaviour sometimes arises, note that behaviour often has *consequences* (Figure 1.13a). If these are such as to alter the future tendency to show the behaviour, they are said to be 'instrumental' in the future outcome. One consequence has an effect termed **reinforcement** (see Figure 1.13b), which can be exemplified as follows using experimental animals.

A rat is placed at the start of a maze and slowly finds its way to the goal of the maze, where it gets a pellet of food. Getting food is conditional upon running through the maze. The behaviour of the rat is *instrumental* in getting the food. Unlike with Pavlov's dog, the events are not simply in the hands of the experimenter. If the rat subsequently runs faster and makes fewer errors in the maze, it would be said that the food has reinforced its running. If the reinforcement (in this case the food) is omitted, in time the rat will stop running through the maze and this piece of behaviour is said to have 'extinguished'.

Now consider an example concerning humans. Suppose that a new child arrives in school and that a psychologist surreptitiously observes the situation. First, he simply observes and records the frequency with which various behaviours occur, giving a baseline measure. Suppose that the child misbehaves and the consequence is that the teacher tells him/her to behave properly. However, over days, the child shows an increasing number of incidents of bad behaviour. The teacher is puzzled, supposing that her critical remarks, described as a form of punishment, should lower the tendency to misbehave.

So, the psychologist suggests that the teacher ignores the child's interruptions. Suppose that they then reduce in frequency. The psychologist concludes that, rather than punishing, the teacher's remarks were *reinforcing* the child's behaviour, i.e. making disruption more likely to occur. This was presumably because the child earned attention. Removal of the remarks constitutes applying 'extinction conditions'. If attention is maintaining the disruptive behaviour, then, by definition, with the removal of attention, it will exhibit 'extinction'.

An important point is that reinforcement does not need to be given in a deliberate way (though sometimes it is). Of course, the teacher did not set out to reinforce the bad behaviour; it was quite inadvertent.

■   Might the principle of reinforcement be applied to Mary's drug-taking?

□   This behaviour has the consequence of lifting negative mood. If any bodily symptoms of withdrawal are present, these are also corrected. These consequences appear to increase the future tendency to repeat this behaviour and would be described as 'reinforcing'.

For Mary, and indeed all individuals who are addicted to a drug of some form, these are *immediate* consequences of taking the drug. Significant events that immediately follow an action are potentially powerful reinforcers. Standing outside the situation, one might see that a longer-term consequence of Mary's drug-taking is to put her on the treadmill of addiction and despair. However, long-term consequences do not lock into association with behaviour as strongly as do immediate consequences.

Based upon principles of instrumental conditioning, how might Mary be helped to break her habit? One approach has been to try to alter the immediate ('reinforcing') consequences of drug-taking by prescribing medication that blocks the 'high'. As you might have guessed, a problem is in persuading the person to try this treatment and remain using it until drug-taking extinguishes. You will learn more about treating addiction in Book 3.

An understanding of reinforcement triggers thinking about mental ill-health in useful ways. Researchers and therapists, as well as loved ones and colleagues, can be on guard for subtle and often unexpected reinforcement. For example, someone with a phobia about leaving their apartment might find this inadvertently reinforced by the presence of well-meaning people who start to visit them on hearing of the problem.

As another example, people in distress sometimes perform self-mutilation. Apart from a plea for help, psychologists propose that the harm might have reinforcing consequences such as 'anger lowering'; that is, changes that increase the future tendency to do harm (Gratz, 2003). Considering the biological basis of this reinforcement, in at least some people, self-harm appears to stimulate the release of neurochemicals that have beneficial effects on emotional state. These are described in Chapter 2.

1.4 Final word

This chapter has shown where both personal narratives and objective evidence can be used to inform understanding of mental distress. It has introduced you to some key concepts and ways of thinking about mental health including the biomedical and biopsychosocial models. The next chapter will look in more detail at the biological underpinnings of mental health and ill-health, laying the groundwork for an understanding of the links between mind and brain which will be explored throughout the rest of SDK228. As you move on to Chapter 2, however, you should not forget the biopsychosocial model that has been discussed here, which suggests that other factors – those beyond the brain–mind relationship – are equally important in understanding mental ill-health and mental well-being.

1.5 Summary of Chapter 1

- In assessing mental health and ill-health, both subjective and objective measures can be used.

- Use of the term 'abnormality' raises profound issues and is usually used to indicate a deviation from a desired state of mental health.

- Biological, psychological and social factors are involved in mental health and ill-health.

- A biomedical model defines diseases in terms of identifiable disturbances of the body.

- A biopsychosocial perspective considers interdependent biological, psychological and social factors as equally important in explaining mental health and ill-health.

- The term 'holism' refers to taking all types of evidence into account and is implicit in a biopsychosocial perspective.

- The term 'reductionism' refers to seeking an explanation of events by looking at only one level; in the case of behaviour and mind this is usually the biological level.

- According to a biomedical model, and also a biopsychosocial model, it is assumed that, for every mental event, there exists a corresponding brain event.

- Whether a treatment for mental distress is biological, psychological or social, it is assumed that, for any change, both subjective experience and brain events are affected.

- Where beneficial effects derive from expectations about a treatment, this is termed a 'placebo effect'.

- Positive psychology emphasises maintaining psychological health rather than simply treating ill-health.

- A comparison of the occurrence of disorders in different populations can be a fruitful source of speculation on their causes.

- Drugs can alter the brain processes that are associated with distressing cognitions.

- A cognitive form of therapy targets cognitions by challenging their validity.

- In classical conditioning, associations are formed between significant events and neutral stimuli. In instrumental conditioning, reinforcement increases the frequency of showing a particular behaviour.

1.6 Learning outcomes

LO 1.1 Outline the meaning of 'mental disorder', the history of treating it and how treatments relate to an understanding of the causes of disorder. (KU4, CS5)

LO 1.2 Describe what is meant by a biopsychosocial approach to understanding mental health and ill-health. (KU3, CS5, KS3)

LO 1.3 Describe some psychological and biological interventions for distress and explain why their effects should not be dichotomised in terms of *either* biological *or* psychological. (KU3, CS5, KS3)

LO 1.4 Explain what is meant by the term 'brain–mind'. (KU3, KU4)

1.7 Self-assessment questions

SAQ 1.1 (LOs 1.1, 1.2, 1.3 and 1.4)

A person having an intense fear of a particular object or situation is described as being 'phobic'. Helen has a phobia about open spaces and finds it hard to leave her house. The therapist encourages her to make brief guided excursions outside. What are possible subjective and objective measures of such a phobia and recovery from it?

SAQ 1.2 (LOs 1.1, 1.2 and 1.3)

Employ the terms 'reductionist' and 'biopsychosocial' with reference to Neha's depression. Show where caution is needed in a reductionist account.

SAQ 1.3 (LO 1.1)

José is a compulsive checker, spending two hours each night checking that windows are locked. When he comes to bed, his wife gives him reassurance that everything is secure. How might his wife's behaviour be counter-productive?

Chapter 2 Bodies, brains, behaviour and minds

Frederick Toates

2.1 Introduction

Chapter 1 described how insight can be gained into the possible determinants of mental health and ill-health by investigating the social context, brain, behaviour and minds of individuals affected by mental distress or who show a strong sense of mental well-being. Chapter 2 now narrows the focus to the brain and biology. However, in reading the chapter you should not lose sight of the biopsychosocial perspective and the fact that abnormal conditions of the brain reflect only one part of this holistic approach to mental health.

At all times during life, the brain shows activity in the form of electrical waves and pulses, which can be detected by measuring devices. Activity patterns of the brains of people who have been diagnosed with, say, depression, can be compared with the patterns of those who do not have this condition and differences noted. Further insight can be gained from a comparison of the brains of people when they are suffering from a mental health condition as compared with when they have recovered. In this way, knowledge is obtained on how treatments work, in terms of changing the activity pattern of the brain and the associated mental state.

Of course, the brain does not exist in isolation. Rather, it has interdependence with other parts of the body. Hence, an understanding of the brain will need to be generated in the context of its links with other regions.

The body can be classified and described in a number of ways. One is to focus upon its different **organs**. An organ is a structure of the body that serves a particular function. Examples include the heart, lungs and brain. Our principal concern is with the brain but at times we will need to understand its interactions with other organs.

Another way of describing the body is in terms of 'systems', such as the circulatory system, which comprises the blood, heart and blood vessels. The principal system of interest in SDK228 is the **nervous system**, highlighted in Figure 2.1. The nervous system is a part of the body concerned with control and communication. As you can see, the brain is part of the nervous system. Figure 2.1 highlights a part of the nervous system termed the **central nervous system** (often abbreviated as the CNS), made up from the brain and the spinal cord. The remainder of the nervous system is termed 'the peripheral nervous system'.

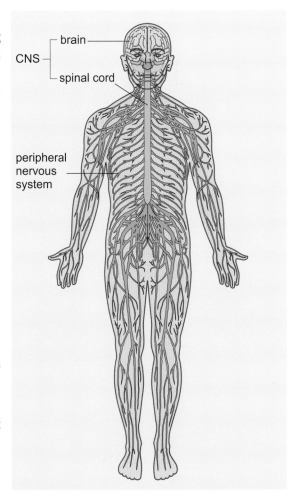

Figure 2.1 The nervous system, showing the central nervous system coloured brown and the peripheral nervous system coloured green.

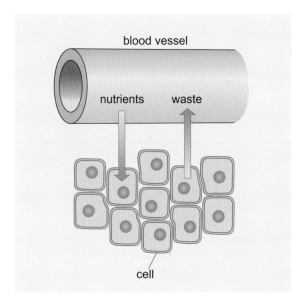

Figure 2.2 Some cells of the body, showing the blood supply to them.

As an example of an interaction, the circulatory system and the nervous system are strongly interdependent. The circulatory system brings blood to the brain and carries blood away from it. Reciprocally, the brain affects the circulatory system (e.g. to accelerate the heart rate at times of threat), as Jim (the man whose heart attack was described in Chapter 1) is slowly coming to appreciate.

Finally, each organ is made up of many billions of minute components, called **cells**. The cell is the basic structural unit of all living things. The estimate of the number of cells in the brain is many billions. Cells require a supply of blood to bring nutrients and oxygen to them and to carry waste products away from them (Figure 2.2).

The nervous system interacts with the **endocrine system**, parts of which are shown in Figure 2.3 as **glands**. The endocrine system is one of the body's systems that serves the role of signalling and it consists of, amongst other things, various **hormones**. These are chemicals secreted into the blood by

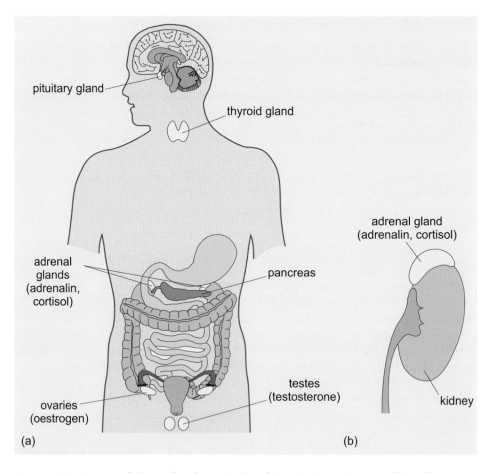

Figure 2.3 Some of the endocrine glands of the body and some of the hormones that they produce.

glands (and other sources of secretion) and carried in the blood. Activity in particular regions of the brain influences the secretion of certain hormones.

Hormones exert effects throughout the body, such as to cause the heart to accelerate its beat at times of anger. Reciprocally, by their actions on the brain, hormones affect our mental states and behaviour. Thus, mental health and ill-health are to some extent reflected in the levels of particular hormones in the body.

This chapter looks at how the brain works, whilst linking this to the mind, behaviour and the body outside of the brain. It will start by looking at the gross anatomy and function of the brain and then consider the cells of which it is composed.

2.2 The study of whole brains

2.2.1 What does the brain do?

Figure 2.4 is a side view of a human brain, showing the pattern of the outside of the brain, made up of grooves that give it an appearance like a walnut. Figure 2.5 shows a front view, where you can see that it is in part divided into two halves, termed **hemispheres**.

What exactly do brains do? In (very!) short, brains *process information* and *control behaviour*.

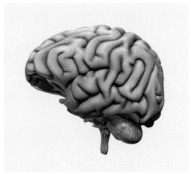

Figure 2.4 Side view of the human brain.

Activity 2.1 Exemplifying action

(LO 2.2) Allow 5 minutes

Count to ten and, when you reach ten, raise a finger in the air. Note down what was involved in this action.

How is such action exerted? There are communication channels from the eyes to the brain and between the brain and the muscles, information being sent along these. The details are explained shortly.

Particular parts of the brain serve particular roles in behaviour and scientists are able, up to a point, to associate these parts with their role. Correspondingly, they can sometimes associate damage to these parts with disruption to particular features of behaviour. Figure 2.6 shows the vessels ('arteries') that convey blood to the brain. If one of these vessels is damaged or blocked, there is a reduction in blood supply to the local brain region, with the resultant death of cells and loss of function. For example, the blood vessel at the point marked X might be disrupted with an associated loss of cells in the vicinity of X. A region in the left hemisphere has a particular responsibility for speech. If this region is disrupted, as in a stroke, there will be a disruption to speech.

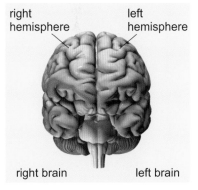

right hemisphere   left hemisphere

right brain   left brain

Figure 2.5 Front view of the human brain.

A stroke arises from blockage of one of the brain's blood vessels or rupture of the wall of a vessel so that blood cannot get to the cells in part of the brain; speech can be severely impaired.

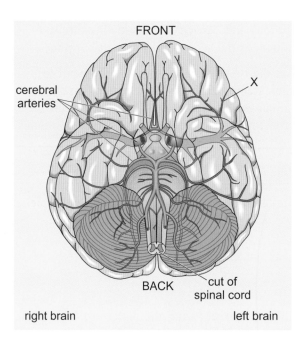

Figure 2.6 The arteries of the brain.

In the condition termed 'dementia', a form of which Mark (Chapter 1) exhibits, there is damage to parts of the brain (discussed in detail in Book 4). Figure 2.7 shows the outside appearance of a normal brain and that of a person who had severe dementia. The shrinkage of regions in the affected brain is evident and there would be an associated loss of function in terms of memory amongst other things.

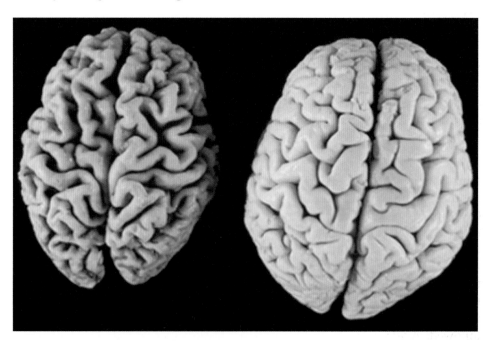

Figure 2.7 Brain of a patient who had a severe form of dementia (left) as compared with a normal brain (right).

2.2.2 Patterns of activity of the brain

Measuring activity

As shown in Figure 2.8, electrodes can be attached to the head enabling electrical activity in the brain regions below each electrode to be measured.

This technique is known as **electroencephalography** and the record obtained is called an **electroencephalogram** (the abbreviation for both terms is EEG). The activity in the outer region of the brain will dominate the signals that are measured. Changes in this activity can be observed: for example, as the person passes from waking through shallow sleep and into deep sleep. Other techniques can be used to measure activity in deeper regions, to which the discussion now turns.

Electrodes are small pieces of metal that are attached to the skin of the head and have wires connected to them. The electrodes detect electrical signals in the brain immediately beneath the electrode and the wires convey this signal to the recording apparatus.

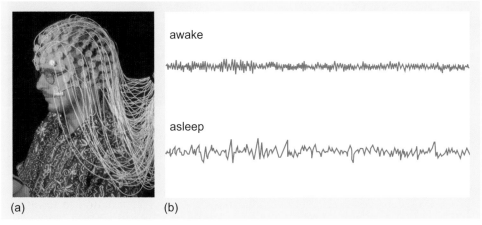

(a) (b)

Figure 2.8 Electroencephalography: (a) the technique; (b) a recording, termed an electroencephalogram.

All the cells of the body require a supply of nutrients and oxygen in order to function and these are supplied by the blood (Figure 2.2). Suppose that a part of the brain becomes strongly activated during performance of a task. So, the demand for nutrients and oxygen in that region increases and the arteries supplying this region increase in diameter, thereby increasing blood flow. These local adjustments to blood vessels occur automatically.

By using particular techniques that come under the broad heading of **neuroimaging**, it is possible to obtain a measure of the blood that flows to regions of the brain and to monitor changes in this blood flow distribution (Figure 2.9). Neuroimaging consists of placing a person's head in an apparatus that detects the flow of blood. This produces a map of the brain with different regions indicated in terms of the amount of blood that flows in them. Changes in blood flow can then be observed whilst the person performs particular tasks, in so far as these can be done whilst the person lies still and horizontal in the apparatus. In one technique, termed 'PET' for short, a radioactive tracer is injected into the blood and the location of the tracer in the brain can be followed. A way of representing brain activity detected in this way is shown in Figure 2.9b. As more blood flows to a region (upper image), so the colour associated with the representation of that region changes, i.e. there are more areas of yellow and red. It is possible to relate two of the cases described in Chapter 1 to activity in different brain regions, as will now be shown.

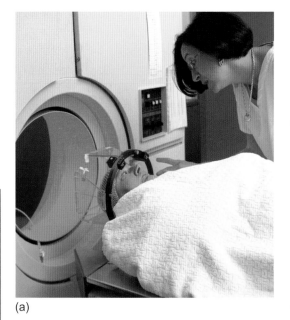
(a)

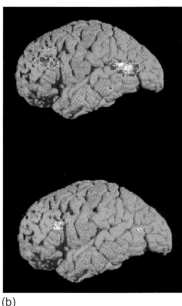
(b)

Figure 2.9 Neuroimaging: (a) the technique; (b) an image.

Gaining objective evidence of 'voices in the head'

Suppose that a person is set a cognitive task of listening to spoken words and imagining a synonym of the word heard. There will be an increase in the flow of blood to those brain regions involved in listening to speech, these being mainly in the left hemisphere of the brain. An image of the brain performing such a task can be compared with that of people who have a condition in which they report 'hearing voices' that are not actually present. In this case, there is activity in those brain regions that would normally be involved in processing speech (Figure 2.10). This gives a biological embodiment of the experience ('objective evidence') and suggests important similarities in the bases of 'hearing voices' that are not there and hearing real voices. Angie (Chapter 1) might be tested in this way and would possibly obtain some comfort in establishing that she is not faking and indeed has a condition with a measurable basis in the brain.

Measuring changes associated with therapy

Chapter 1 described John, who has obsessive–compulsive disorder (OCD). Research has observed characteristic patterns of blood flow in particular regions of the brains of people with this condition. A number of pieces of evidence lead to the conclusion that, in particular, abnormal activity levels in two strongly interacting regions of the brain are implicated in OCD, as follows.

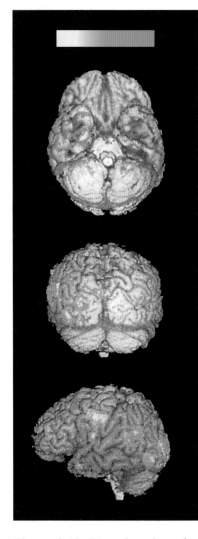

Figure 2.10 Neuroimaging of the brain of a person with auditory and visual hallucinations. Red and yellow indicate areas of particular activity.

The word **cortex** means 'bark', as in the bark of a tree, and it refers to the outer layer of the brain (Figure 2.11). Figure 2.12 highlights a region of cortex at the front of the brain, termed the prefrontal cortex (PFC). A part of the PFC forms a focus in the study of OCD – the orbitofrontal cortex (OFC), which is the lowest part of the blue area in Figure 2.12a and b. Using a PET scan, increased blood flow and use of metabolic fuel (glucose) in the PFC has been found in people with OCD, as compared to people without (Biver et al., 1995). Another brain region, the caudate nucleus (Figure 2.11), which is deep within the brain, also exhibits elevated activity in OCD. There is a positive relationship between the elevation in activity in these regions and the severity of OCD. Figure 2.13a compares activity in the brains of a person without OCD and a person with OCD. The activity in the caudate nucleus on the right side of the brain (rCd) is highlighted in Figure 2.13b, comparing a person with OCD before and after treatment.

The amount of metabolic fuel used gives a measure of the activity of the part of the brain under consideration.

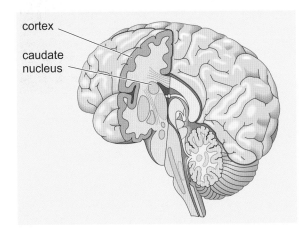

Figure 2.11 View of the brain after part of the left hemisphere is cut away.

In one study, people with OCD were given either drug therapy or **behaviour therapy**. Behaviour therapy consisted of gradual exposure to the object of their fear, as in the case of John in Chapter 1. Under each treatment, a lowering of metabolic activity in the caudate nucleus in the right brain was found (Baxter et al., 1992). Those who improved as a result of treatment were compared with two other groups: those who were not responsive to the treatment, and people without OCD. The results are shown in Figure 2.14, each triangle corresponding to one individual.

■ What does this diagram show?

□ Those who improved with treatment, of either form, showed reduced metabolic activity in the right caudate nucleus. Those who failed to respond to treatment showed no change – a similar result to people not having OCD.

Box 2.1 describes how hypotheses concerning disorders such as OCD are constructed and tested, as in the study by Baxter et al.

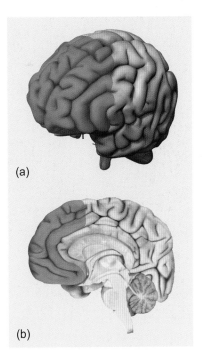

Figure 2.12 The brain, highlighting (blue) the prefrontal cortex. (a) External view; (b) cross-sectional view.

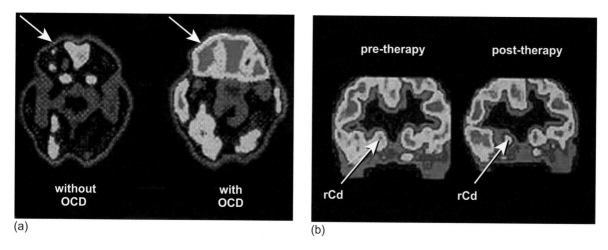

Figure 2.13 Neuroimaging of the brain by means of the PET. (a) Scan of person without OCD as compared with a person with OCD. The arrow points to orbitofrontal cortex. (b) Scan of person with OCD before and after successful treatment. rCd refers to the caudate nucleus on the right side of the brain.

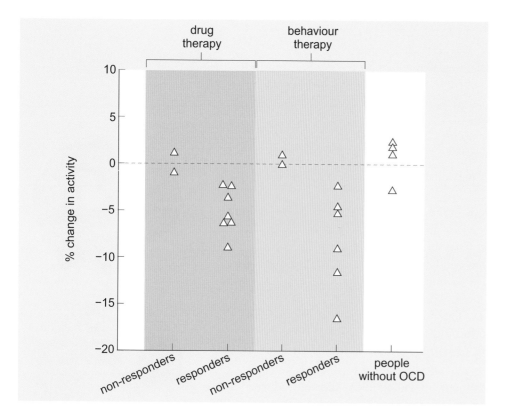

Figure 2.14 The percentage change in metabolic activity of the right caudate nucleus in people with OCD who were responders or non-responders to either drug therapy or behaviour therapy, as well as in people without OCD.

Box 2.1 Research Methods: Hypothesis testing

As mentioned in Box 1.1, experiments are performed on groups of individuals to provide quantifiable data that supports or refutes an idea or an observation. In order to perform an experiment, researchers must first devise what is called an **experimental hypothesis**. This arises as a result of observations of phenomena in brain and behaviour as well as putting these observations into the context of some fundamental assumptions. The OCD studies described in Section 2.2.2 can be used to illustrate how observations and assumptions come together in devising an experimental hypothesis. A fundamental assumption would be that:

- mental events correspond to events in the brain.

Three observations from previous studies would be that:

- people showing OCD have abnormal patterns of activity in various regions of their brains, including the caudate nucleus (Figure 2.13a)
- drug therapy can alleviate the distress of OCD
- behaviour therapy can alleviate the distress of OCD.

The above assumption and these observations would lead to the general idea that therapies for OCD might have effects in areas of the brain showing abnormal activity in OCD. As a specific example, an experimental hypothesis for a study investigating the effects of drug therapy on OCD could be devised based on the following aim: to test whether drug therapy affects the activity of the caudate nucleus in the brains of people with OCD. An experimental hypothesis always predicts a difference of some kind between two or more conditions (in this case, the conditions are before and after therapy and the same participants are used in the two conditions). Therefore an appropriately worded experimental hypothesis for the study would be 'there will be *a difference* between the activity of the caudate nucleus in the brains of people with OCD before and after drug therapy'. Figure 2.13b shows a PET scan of a person with OCD before and after successful drug therapy. To recap: the experimental hypothesis predicts that there will be a difference in activity of the caudate nucleus in the brains of people with OCD before and after drug therapy.

The converse of the experimental hypothesis is the **null hypothesis**. For our example study, this would be worded as follows 'there will be *no difference* between the activity of the caudate nucleus in the brains of people with OCD before and after drug therapy'. Thus the null hypothesis always predicts no difference between experimental conditions. Note that the null hypothesis should always be given as well as the experimental hypothesis. At the end of an experiment, a decision is made about whether to accept or reject the null hypothesis on the basis of statistical calculations. The question under investigation is whether therapy causes changes in the brain. In other words, does the outcome depend on whether therapy had or had not been administered? The administration of therapy is the variable that the experimenter has control over and is termed the **independent variable**. In another experiment, the two types of therapy could be compared, in which case the independent variable would be the type of therapy. The outcome that is measured in an experiment is termed the **dependent variable**. This graph shows that the independent variable – that is, the administration of therapy – does appear to have an effect on the dependent variable of metabolic rate, but only in the people that responded to the treatment.

In some instances in mental health studies this situation can be complicated when the aim of a study is to assess whether a new potential therapy is *as effective* as an existing therapy. One might imagine that the new drug therapy for OCD that has just been discussed could be compared with an existing and effective behavioural therapy for OCD which is known to alter activity in the caudate nucleus. In this case, in comparing the activity of the caudate nucleus in participants receiving the existing behavioural therapy with participants receiving the new drug therapy, the researchers are actually expecting that the null hypothesis will be supported by their findings. The null hypothesis would state 'there will be no difference in the activity of the caudate nucleus in people with OCD receiving the existing behavioural therapy compared to people with OCD receiving drug therapy'. Take care here however. This does *not* mean that the null hypothesis now becomes the experimental hypothesis because the over-riding rule is that the experimental hypothesis *always* predicts a difference between the conditions of the independent variable. This is the case even if researchers actually expect to find the opposite. Thus, in this fictitious example, the experimental hypothesis would be 'there will be a difference in the activity of the caudate nucleus in people with OCD receiving behavioural therapy compared to people receiving drug therapy'.

One particular treatment for OCD is termed **brain lock** and is based upon the following principle (Schwartz, 1996). People with OCD are taught how to reinterpret obsessive thoughts and to consider them, not as deserving the usual compulsive response, but as a disorder of the *brain*. They are taught the slogan 'it's not me, it's my OCD' and are shown brain images of other people, before and after treatment. So, understanding the biological roots of the disorder can help people to combat it. The treatment does not directly target the brain but targets patterns of thought and behaviour. Yet, when it is successful, it has results that can be measured in terms of the brain's activity. This again highlights the interdependence of brain and mind. In the most extreme cases, OCD totally incapacitates the individual and as a last resort, surgical interventions can be made in the form of destruction of a small amount of tissue within the implicated parts of the PFC (Irle et al., 1998). Improvements in terms of reported symptoms are found following this intervention. A reduction in activity in the PFC and caudate nucleus is seen, comparable to the result for successful treatment of OCD by either drugs or behaviour therapy (Biver et al., 1995). However, assessment of the outcome is not easy: there is difficulty in finding suitable participants for the control group (see Box 2.2).

■ Why do you suppose that this is so?

□ One needs people having equal severity of OCD but, for some reason, not receiving the operation.

From looking at activity patterns in the brains of people with OCD, researchers are able to understand better the normal roles of the brain regions involved. The caudate nucleus controls sequences of action, switching between different activities and probably also between different patterns of thought. In OCD, it gets 'stuck in a groove'. The PFC underlies decision-making and its overactivity in OCD appears to indicate a role in trying endlessly to solve an insoluble problem and to get the corresponding behaviour 'out of the groove'. Another study which monitored changes in brain activity by means of neuroimaging looked at people with a spider phobia as they underwent behaviour therapy (Paquette et al., 2003). The patients experienced what is known as 'graded exposure'. **Graded exposure** refers to a slow and gradual exposure to stimuli that are the object of fear. Firstly, exposure in this study was to stimuli that evoke relatively low levels of fear, such as a distant picture of a spider. The patients were then exposed to closer images, followed by a model spider in the distance and, ultimately, contact with real spiders. Over the course of exposure, enormous improvement was shown, as indexed by subjective reports of reduction in fear. Finally, patients were able to touch real spiders. Brain neuroimaging was carried out before and after therapy.

To detect changes in activity of the brain during exposure to the phobic object, a source of comparison is needed.

■ What would be a suitable source of comparison?

□ People with phobias could be compared with people without phobia.

Also, the people with phobias were compared under the condition of triggering fear (spider stimulus) and when they viewed a 'neutral stimulus' – that is, one that triggered no subjective fear (a butterfly). Given that all the cells of the brain use fuel all the time, researchers are interested in changes in activity relative to another condition. So, brain activity for viewing the spider is compared to that for the viewing the butterfly before and after completion of therapy. In a number of brain regions, marked differences in the form of activation were seen comparing spider and butterfly conditions prior to therapy but not after therapy. One such region is the prefrontal cortex in the right hemisphere of the brain (Figure 2.12). Such studies on people with OCD and phobias reveal two very important properties of the brain:

• Even when an intervention is psychological, it has consequences for brain and behaviour.

• The brain exhibits **plasticity**: over time, it can change as a result of the situation to which the person is exposed.

It is believed that the brain changes some of the connections between its cells (breaking some connections and forming new connections elsewhere). These changes underlie the changes in observed brain activity.

Measuring hemispheric differences and mood

The term **affective style** refers to a person's way of reacting emotionally to events in the world. It highlights differences between individuals in their general mood and emotional reaction to events. Some researchers assume that such differences in psychology are reflected in differences in the brain's emotion systems between individuals (Davidson, 2005). For example, one might expect evidence of differences in emotion in people leading as different lives as Mary and Claudia (Chapter 1). The biological basis of mood and emotion can be established by means of studies of brain activity in the following groups of people:

- those with no known brain damage or obvious behavioural disturbance
- those showing emotional disturbance
- those with known damage to the brain.

Figure 2.12 shows the prefrontal cortex. As was described, there is activation of this region on the right side in people with spider phobias when confronting spiders. Evidence suggests that parts of this structure in both hemispheres participate in emotion (Davidson, 2005). It points to a different role in emotion between the left and right hemispheres. A caution needs immediately to be sounded and it has general relevance to the study of the brain: although the identified brain region participates in emotion, it does not do so in isolation. It is not a unique and isolated 'seat of emotion'. Rather, emotion arises from interacting brain regions, of which the PFC is just one. None the less, the study of this region has given insights particularly into the basis of differences in affective style between individuals.

The left PFC appears to participate most strongly in *positive* emotion and mood. Damage there (e.g. in a stroke) increases the tendency to depression. When a positive mood is induced by showing a happy film, there is increased activity in the left PFC. By contrast, when a *negative* mood is induced, there is increased activity in the right PFC. Using the technique of EEG, when participants in a research study are given reward (gain of money), activation is seen in the left hemisphere, whereas when they are given punishment (loss of money), activation is seen in the right hemisphere (Sobotka et al., 1992).

Results from brain neuroimaging dovetail with those obtained from EEG. As noted with spider phobia, it is possible to study people with particular anxiety conditions as they confront the trigger to their anxiety (Davidson, 2005). For example, when people with a social phobia contemplate making a speech, they show a particular activation of the right PFC. This result fits with the study of spider phobia, described earlier. Using EEG, Davidson and Fox (1989) first measured the baseline activity levels of the PFC in 10-month-old human infants. They then observed the infants' reactions to separation from the mother. Those infants who cried in this situation tended to be ones showing greater baseline right-sided activity relative to the left side. As a comparison, a region of cortex further towards the back of the brain was also examined and found not to be different in activity when crying and non-crying babies were compared.

Such results raise the possibility that interventions that successfully improve a person's psychological state might be accompanied by a relative shift of activation from right to left PFC. A population of participants is needed, who are divided into two groups, termed 'experimentals' and 'controls' (see Box 2.2). The 'experimentals' would receive therapeutic intervention, whereas the 'controls' would not. In such a study, over an eight-week period, experimentals received a training programme in meditation, a procedure associated with increases in subjective well-being (Davidson et al., 2003). It was found that, compared to controls, the experimentals showed a significant increase in activation of the left PFC. Interestingly, the Dalai Lama makes a point congruent with such studies (Dalai Lama and Cutler, 1998):

> The systematic training of the mind – the cultivation of happiness, the genuine inner transformation by deliberately selecting and focusing on positive mental states and challenging negative mental states – is possible because of the very structure and function of the brain … But the wiring in our brains is not static, not irrevocably fixed. Our brains are also adaptable.

Such change in the brain is an example of a property of the brain that has already been described, namely *plasticity*. It is now time to look in more detail at what is meant by the expressions 'wiring' of the brain and brain activity.

Box 2.2 Research Methods: Participants in experiments

It is very important that participants in experiments are carefully selected according to predefined criteria. For example, in the OCD experiment described in Box 2.1, the criteria might be a particular type of OCD or a particular level of severity of symptoms. Defining the population of participants in this way reduces variation between individuals, but it also means that the results are only applicable to that particular population. Once the population is defined, it is necessary to select a sample of participants that are representative of that population. Decisions need to be made about how to select participants and how many participants should be included in the study. In Section 2.2.2, a study is described that measures activation in the left PFC in response to a period of meditation. In this experiment, there is an **experimental condition** in which participants are asked to practise meditation over a period of time and a **control condition** in which meditation is not practised. The outcome found in the experimental condition is compared against that for the control condition. Exactly what the participants in the control group would be asked to do is a difficult question to resolve. They might be asked simply to read a book for the same amount of time each day that those in the experimental group are spending in meditation.

At the start of the experiment, a measure would be made of brain activity. At the end of this period, the activity of the brains of the participants would again be measured and any differences over the time period noted. The two conditions would then be compared. It is necessary to employ a control condition in order to be sure that any apparent effect of manipulating the independent variable (practising meditation) really was due to this factor. For example, over the period of time when meditation was being practised, it could be that brains might naturally change their activity for reasons unrelated to the meditation (e.g. a change in the weather over this period of time).

In the case described, the study compares results from two groups of people and is termed a **between-participants design**. Participants from the defined population must be carefully allocated to the two conditions. This can be done randomly, so, for example 20 participants are selected and 10 allocated at random to the experimental condition and 10 to the control condition. A variation of a between-participants design is one where participants are matched for characteristics such as age or gender so that each participant has a matched participant in the other condition. It is still necessary to randomly allocate these matched participants to the two conditions.

2.3 The cells that make up the brain and their connections

Having discussed brains and activity in brain regions, it is now time to look on a microscopic scale at the cells that make up the brain. Electrical activity of the brain, as seen on a gross scale in the EEG (Figure 2.8b), reflects the electrical activity of millions of individual cells that lie under the location of the electrodes. A similar principle applies to the technique of neuroimaging. For example, a difference over time in activity in a brain region is a reflection of the combined differences in activity of the millions of cells in this region.

2.3.1 Neurons and action potentials

There are different types of cell found in the brain but one type in particular is the object of interest here: the **neuron**. Neurons transmit messages, both (i) within the nervous system and (ii) between the nervous system and other parts of the body. They also process information. In doing Activity 2.1, when you raised your finger, the message to your muscles to contract was conveyed from the brain by particular neurons (Figure 2.15a). First, neuron 1 conveys the message from the brain and then the message is passed on to neuron 2 to be conveyed to the muscle. In reality, a large number of neurons like these two would be involved, all packed side-by-side as in a cable, but the figure shows only two representative neurons.

How is the message conveyed? It travels in the form of pulses of electricity (voltage) termed **action potentials**. Suppose that you make the decision to raise your finger. Action potentials are produced in the regions of the brain that control the muscles lifting the finger (Figure 2.15b). Action potentials are transmitted along neurons to the muscle and, when they arrive, the muscle is caused to contract, raising the finger.

A principal language of the nervous system is the *frequency* with which action potentials occur. In Figure 2.16, note the increase in the contraction of the muscle. This arises because of an increase in frequency of action potentials in those neurons that activate it. Any given action potential is exactly like any

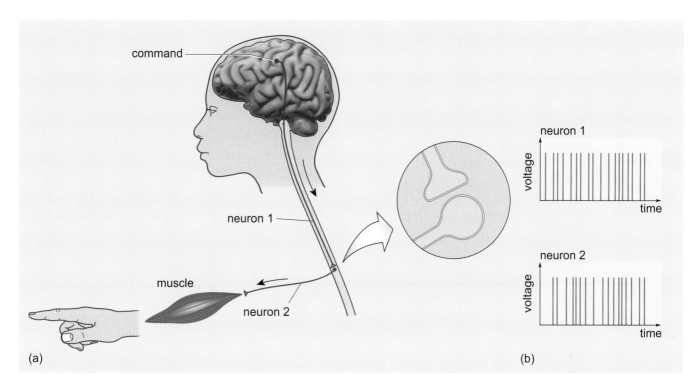

Figure 2.15 Activation of a muscle. (a) Neurons that activate the muscle. (b) Record of action potentials in these neurons.

other – they do not change shape or size. In a given neuron, they all travel at the same speed.

Figure 2.1 showed the whole nervous system. As part of the CNS, the spinal cord is located within the backbone and it consists of billions of neurons, which, amongst other things, transmit action potentials up and down, between the brain and lower parts of the body. In Figure 2.15, the lower part of neuron 1 lies within the spinal cord and so does the junction with neuron 2.

In Figure 2.15, action potentials in neuron 1 trigger further action potentials in neuron 2, an example of **excitation**. Note the small gap between the two neurons (shown magnified) and between neuron 2 and the muscle. You might like to reflect for a moment on how an action potential in neuron 1 can cause an action potential in neuron 2 and how an action potential in neuron 2 can excite the muscle. The next section describes how it really happens.

2.3.2 The synapse and neurotransmitters

A typical synapse

Figure 2.17 shows an enlarged view of the junction between two neurons, where you can see the gap more clearly. When action potentials arrive at the terminal of neuron 1, they trigger a sequence of events that cause the initiation of further action potentials in neuron 2. How is this possible?

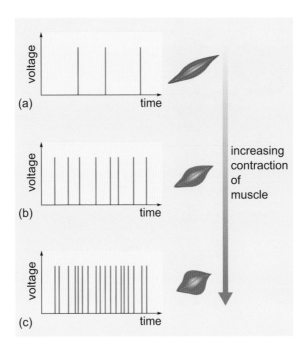

Figure 2.16 The language of the nervous system: frequency of action potentials: (a) low, (b) medium and (c) high, with associated increase in muscle contraction.

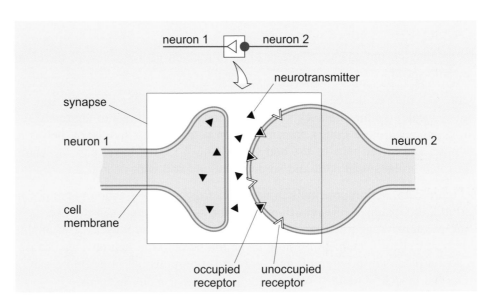

Figure 2.17 A synapse, consisting of the terminal of one neuron, the surface of the next and the gap between them.

Neuron structure, including dendrites, is covered in Activity 2.2.

Note the substance termed **neurotransmitter** that is stored in neuron 1. When an action potential arrives at this terminal, it causes the release of neurotransmitter into the gap. Neurotransmitter then rapidly crosses the gap and attaches to receptors on the surface of neuron 2. These receptors might be sited, for example, on the dendrites of neuron 2. Note that the shape of the neurotransmitter is the same as that of the receptors. If sufficient neurotransmitter occupies the receptors, it will cause a new action potential to arise in neuron 2. You could imagine the synapse shown in Figure 2.17 to be that between neurons 1 and 2 in Figure 2.15.

A similar principle applies to the junction between a neuron and a muscle cell. So, with reference to Figure 2.15, the action potential travels the length of neuron 2, where it triggers the release of neurotransmitter at its terminal. Neurotransmitter crosses the gap and occupies receptors on muscle cells, causing the muscle to contract.

Within the brain, there are billions of synapses formed between neurons. Synapses determine the effects that activity in one neuron has upon another. Consider the statement: 'the PFC of the left hemisphere has a role in positive emotion'. This means that the activity within the neurons in this region forms the physical basis of the subjective experience of positive emotion.

Different types of synapse

So far, this chapter has discussed the excitation of one neuron by another and the excitation of a muscle by a neuron. Excitation is one mode of action but there is another, as shown in Figure 2.18, where excitation is contrasted with **inhibition**. In the case of inhibition, activity of one neuron *suppresses* the activity of another.

Neuron Z (Figure 2.18a) has a spontaneous ('background') activity, meaning that, in the absence of any influence outside the neuron (see graphs (x) and (y)), it produces action potentials at a certain frequency (graph (z)). Neuron X forms an excitatory synapse with neuron Z. Figure 2.18b (graph (z)) shows the result of activity in neuron Z when neuron X is active (graph (x)).

■ What is the effect in terms of activity in neuron Z?

□ Relative to the background activity, there is an *increase* in frequency of action potentials in neuron Z when neuron X is active: the defining criterion of excitation.

Next imagine that neuron X is inactive but neuron Y, which has an inhibitory effect on neuron Z, becomes active. The result in neuron Z is shown in Figure 2.18c.

■ How would you characterise the effect on neuron Z?

□ There is a *reduction* in frequency of action potentials in neuron Z as a result of activity in neuron Y: this is the defining feature of inhibition.

Now suppose that both neuron X and Y are active simultaneously (Figure 2.18d).

■ How would you characterise the effect on neuron Z?

□ The effects of excitation and inhibition will tend to cancel each other out.

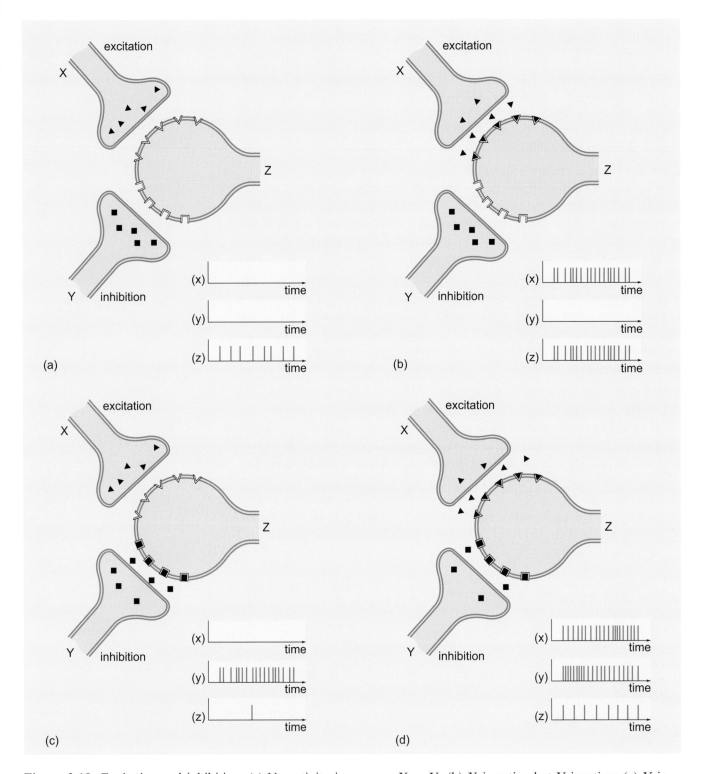

Figure 2.18 Excitation and inhibition. (a) No activity in neurons X or Y; (b) X is active but Y inactive; (c) Y is active but X is inactive; (d) both X and Y are active.

The role of inhibition in the nervous system can be illustrated by familiar processes of mind and behaviour. Often the conditions will be such that action might be expected to be triggered but the action is resisted. You might be trying to lose weight and yet feel tempted by the sight of a cake. The image will set up desire but you resist. There is conflict in your mind, with the urge to eat being inhibited by processes of restraint. If mental processes are embodied in processes in the brain, this suggests the existence of excitation and inhibition, as represented in Figure 2.19. However, don't assume that a decision is based upon the activity of single neurons. Doubtless complex pathways and circuits of thousands of neurons are involved. However, the existence of excitation and inhibition between neurons provides an essential ingredient in the functioning of the brain as a whole.

What determines whether excitation or inhibition at a given synapse will occur? It is the *combination* of neurotransmitter and its receptors. There are various neurotransmitters. Some exert an excitatory effect when they occupy particular receptors, whereas others exert an inhibitory effect. One neurotransmitter amongst others that has a general excitatory effect is termed 'glutamate', whereas one that has a general inhibitory effect is termed 'GABA' (Figure 2.20).

A synapse can be characterised by the type of neurotransmitter that is employed there. For example, one at which glutamate is released and occupies receptors is termed 'glutamatergic'. A neuron that releases glutamate is also known as 'glutamatergic'.

From Figures 2.18 and 2.20, you can see that the relationship of neurotransmitter and receptors is like that of a **lock and key**. A given type of neurotransmitter fits only a particular kind of receptor, as represented by them having the same shape. If a neighbouring neuron has different receptors, this neurotransmitter will not attach to them. An implication of this is shown in Figure 2.21. If a different type of neurotransmitter should diffuse across to another synapse, since it is of a different shape it will not attach to the receptors there. Hence, it will not exert any effect at that synapse. This is a means of avoiding 'cross-talk' between neuronal circuits.

Elimination of neurotransmitter from the synapse

Try again lifting your finger and then after a few seconds decide to lower it, as rapidly as possible (Figure 2.15). In the nervous system, what is the basis for these events? Action potentials were sent along neurons to the muscles controlling the finger. Neurotransmitter was released and it occupied receptors on the muscle, causing it to contract and the finger to rise.

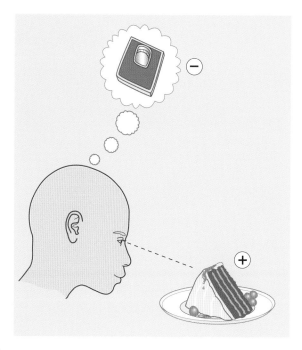

Figure 2.19 Excitation and inhibition of the tendency to feed.

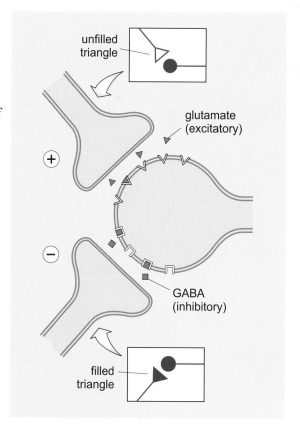

Figure 2.20 Representation of synapses that employ glutamate and GABA.

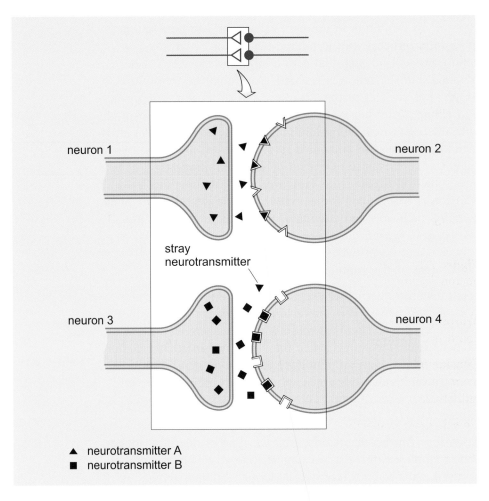

Figure 2.21 The lock-and-key relationship between a particular neurotransmitter and its receptors.

But how did the finger come down again? Why did it not stay permanently in the air? This example illustrates an important general message about communication in the nervous system. There is more than one process involved, but it is useful to focus on just one of them (Figure 2.22).

On making the decision to lower the finger, there is a sudden reduction in the frequency of action potentials in the neurons supplying the muscles that held it up and hence there is a sudden reduction in the amount of transmitter released. What about the transmitter that already occupies the receptors? In fact, neurotransmitter is removed from the synapse immediately after occupying its receptors. In the example shown, the neurotransmitter is broken down into its components, termed **metabolites**. These are inert as far as the synapse is concerned.

A metabolite is a product of the biological breakdown of any larger molecule.

So, when the supply of neurotransmitter is stopped, neurotransmitter is instantly removed from the synapse, as indicated by the speed of fall of your finger. To keep the finger raised would require a continuous release of neurotransmitter exactly matching the rate of removal, triggered by holding the frequency of action potentials at a high level. The removal of

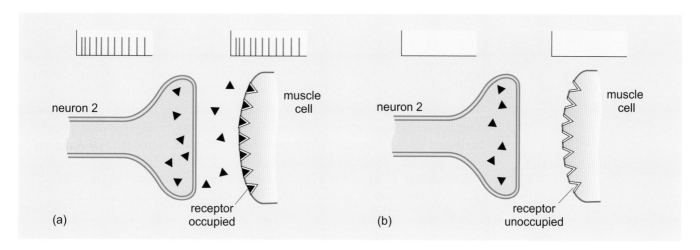

Figure 2.22 Raising and lowering the finger. (a) Activity in neuron 2 excites the muscle. (b) Cessation of activity in neuron 2 and cessation of activation of the muscle.

neurotransmitter from the synapse means that action can be very rapidly controlled. In this case, the muscles can follow commands from the brain.

Considering synapses within the brain, because of elimination of neurotransmitter from the synapse, changes in activity of one neuron can very quickly follow changes in the activity of another.

How is neurotransmitter removed from the synapse? As just noted, in some cases, it is broken down into metabolites by a chemical present at the synapse (Figure 2.23a). However, there is another means of removal, shown in Figure 2.23b. Neurotransmitter is taken back into the neuron that released it, a process termed **reuptake**.

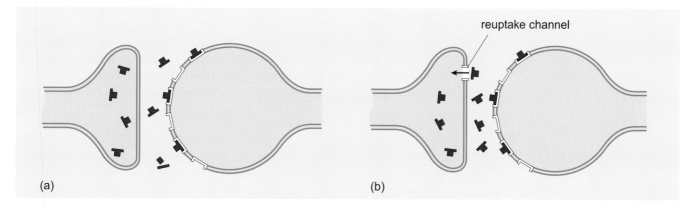

Figure 2.23 Removal of neurotransmitter from a synapse by (a) breakdown into inert components (metabolites) and (b) reuptake.

Activity 2.2 The neuron, action potential and synapse
(LO 2.2) Allow 1 hour

Now would be an ideal time to study the interactive animation 'The neuron, action potential and synapse' in the multimedia map. The animation presents the basics of the nervous system, including structure of the neuron and how synapses work. There are interactive exercises designed to aid your understanding of what the terms 'excitation' and 'inhibition' mean, when applied to the links between neurons. The sequence will also show an animation of synaptic activity.

2.4 Changes in activity at synapses

The basic knowledge of neurotransmitters and synapses just presented is essential for understanding how drugs, legal and illegal, influence the nervous system and thereby the mind and behaviour. Recall the idea that patterns of activity within neurons form the basis of mental states. Drugs change the activity patterns within particular groups of neurons by changing the activity at synapses. Thereby, they change mental states. This section looks in more detail at a few examples of how this happens.

2.4.1 Altering reuptake

SSRIs and depression

In Chapter 1, Neha was described as taking Prozac as an antidepressant. Prozac acts at synapses in the brain that employ the neurotransmitter serotonin. It acts by selectively blocking the reuptake of serotonin, hence it is one of a class of drugs termed **selective serotonin reuptake inhibitors (SSRIs)**. Relative to some other drugs, it is 'selective' in its effects by acting only on serotonin. Figure 2.24 represents the action of an SSRI.

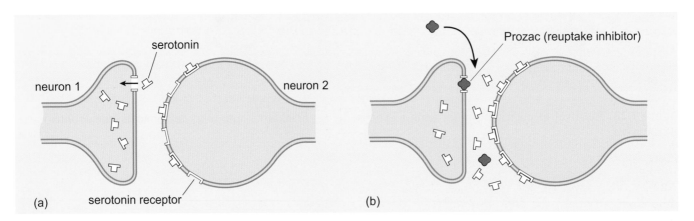

Figure 2.24 The action of a selective serotonin reuptake inhibitor (SSRI). A synapse: (a) without Prozac; (b) with Prozac. Serotonin is represented as a T-shape.

■ What does the figure show?

☐ The level of serotonin in the gap between neurons 1 and 2 increases as a result of the action of Prozac. Correspondingly, the level of occupation of receptors on neuron 2 by serotonin increases.

Because of increased occupation of receptors, the activity of neuron 2 is changed. Exactly how this effect of Prozac on serotonin reuptake exerts its beneficial psychological effect on some people suffering from depression is still not clear and Figure 2.24b, of course, illustrates only an effect at the level of individual neurons. It can be speculated that by altering serotonin levels, the drug alters the balance of activity between certain brain regions (Carver et al., 2008). Those regions that are involved in bringing repetitive ('automatic') negative thoughts to conscious awareness are inhibited.

SSRIs and OCD

Suppose John was prescribed the drug Prozac as a treatment for his OCD. One might speculate as to how a benefit might be felt, along the following lines.

John was described as being in some ambivalence. He knew 'at one level' of his mind that it was extremely unlikely that washing his hands could save his family. Let's suppose that there are particular brain regions, employing particular neurotransmitters, at the basis of such beliefs. On 'the other level' of his mind, this belief did not gain access to the control of his behaviour, which was dominated by another part of his mind that kept telling him that he needed to wash his hands in order to ward off evil. Suppose that there is a corresponding competition within his brain for control of behaviour. As with Neha, it could be that those parts of the brain that are responsible for rational reasoning could be strengthened in their effects by Prozac altering serotonergic activity there.

Side effects of drugs

John was having problems with the medication prescribed for his OCD. It made him sleepy, dizzy and produced a dry mouth. Such unintended effects are known as **side effects**. Taking medicine for mental distress is a 'blunt instrument', something that you will come to appreciate throughout SDK228. The desired aim is to target selectively just the parts of the brain that, it is assumed, are showing malfunction. However, a medicine such as Prozac can never be that selective.

Recall that the addition of '-ergic' to the name of a neurotransmitter makes it an adjective; for example a serotonergic neuron is one that releases serotonin.

There are a number of brain processes that employ serotonergic neurons, including those that control eating and cycles of sleeping and waking. Hence, not only are the brain processes that are the desired target of the drug affected but so too are some others.

Another way in which side effects can arise is shown in Figure 2.25, for the drug clomipramine. This drug also targets serotonergic synapses and is used to treat depression and OCD. Clomipramine is broken down into its component molecules and one of these blocks reuptake of a neurotransmitter that is not

In the American literature, adrenalin and noradrenalin are termed 'epinephrine' and 'norepinephrine', respectively.

the target of therapy: noradrenalin. Altering the activity of noradrenalin produces the side effect of a dry mouth, amongst other things.

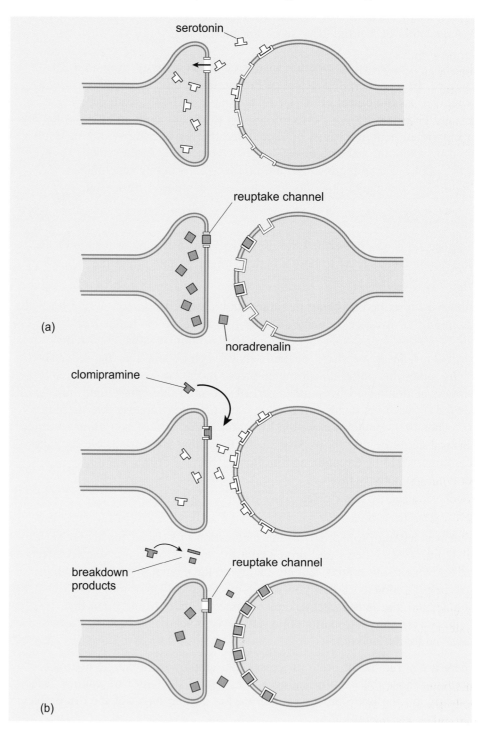

Figure 2.25 The action of clomipramine. (a) Normal serotonergic and noradrenergic synapses; (b) the same synapses with the drug present.

Other drugs exert their effects by occupying receptors for the natural neurotransmitter, to which the discussion now turns.

2.4.2 The occupation of receptors for the natural neurotransmitter

Agonists and antagonists

Suppose that an artificial substance has a shape similar to a natural neurotransmitter. It binds to receptors that would normally be occupied by the natural neurotransmitter. After binding, it can have the effect of mimicking the action of the natural neurotransmitter and is described as an **agonist** to it (Figure 2.26). The agonist might exert a beneficial effect if there is a deficiency in the level of natural neurotransmitter.

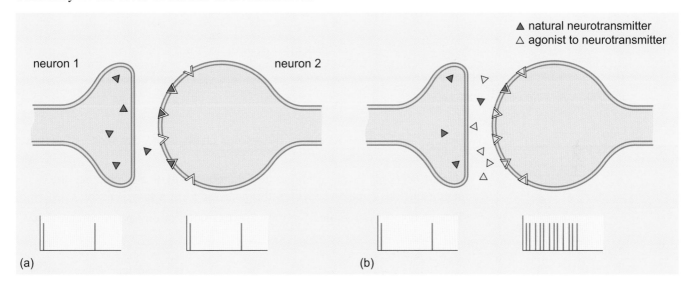

Figure 2.26 The action of an agonist. A synapse: (a) without agonist; (b) with agonist.

By contrast, a different substance might occupy the receptors but have no effect. However, it would block the action of natural neurotransmitter by 'getting in the way'. The substance is serving as an **antagonist** to the natural substance. If an antagonist were found to be helpful in treating a condition, this would suggest that there was excessive activity at the synapses targeted (Figure 2.27).

In addition to their therapeutic role, agonists and antagonists are used extensively as research tools by which the working of parts of the nervous system can be manipulated and the effects observed.

Heroin as an agonist

In Chapter 1, Mary was described as using heroin as 'self-medication'. The body produces natural substances termed **opioids**, for which there are particular receptors on neurons in certain regions of the brain. Heroin is an agonist at such receptors and there are five closely related assumptions that underlie an understanding of its action:

1   There are circuits of neurons in the brain and their activity forms the basis of emotion and mood.

2   On these neurons, there are receptors for opioids.

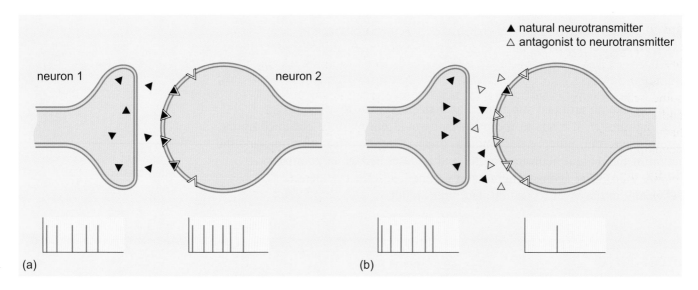

Figure 2.27 The action of an antagonist.

3 Occupation of these receptors by opioids changes the frequency of activity within these circuits.

4 Heroin occupies these receptors and thereby dramatically changes the activity of the circuits of which the neurons form a part (Figure 2.28).

5 This change is felt subjectively as, for example, strong positive emotion.

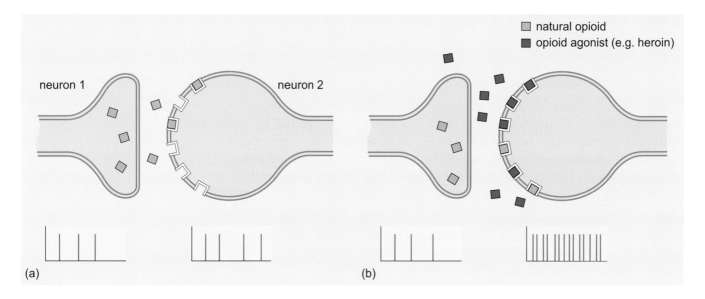

Figure 2.28 Part of a circuit of neurons showing opioid receptors: (a) in the absence of artificial stimulation; (b) in the presence of heroin, an opioid agonist.

Naltrexone as an antagonist

Section 1.3.2 described self-injurious behaviour and the possibility that it might be maintained by its anxiety-reducing consequences – an example of reinforcement. One suggestion is that such behaviour causes the release of opioids which act on receptors in the brain and possibly have some kind of soothing effect. Based on this assumption, the opioid antagonist naltrexone has been tried as a treatment on the assumption that it would block the reinforcing effect (Sandman et al., 2000). Following naltrexone administration, some people dramatically decrease self-injurious behaviour (e.g. self-hitting and self-biting), whereas others do not. This shows that not all drug treatments have the same effect on all individuals, a factor that complicates the development of successful drug treatments for conditions of mental ill-health.

So far, the chapter has considered the nervous system. The next section considers the endocrine system and how it interacts with the nervous system.

2.5 Nervous and endocrine systems in interaction

2.5.1 General principles

A hormone is a chemical released into the bloodstream at one location and carried in the blood to another location, where it exerts an effect. Figure 2.29 compares and contrasts a hormone and a neurotransmitter.

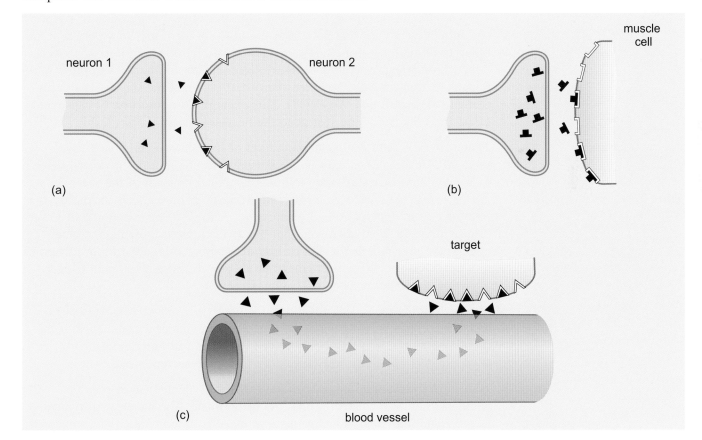

Figure 2.29 Neurotransmitter at (a) a neuron and (b) a muscle, compared with (c) a hormone.

■ What is a similarity between a hormone and a neurotransmitter?

□ Both attach to receptors in a lock-and-key fashion.

■   What is a difference between them?

☐   A neurotransmitter travels the minute distance from the site of its release to its site of action, whereas a hormone is typically distributed widely and travels relatively large distances from the site of its release to its many sites of action throughout the body.

The adrenal gland is also known as the suprarenal gland.

So, the difference between a neurotransmitter and a hormone is not intrinsic to the substance itself but is in its mode of delivery. For example, the substance noradrenalin acts in both roles. Within the brain, it acts as a neurotransmitter at synapses (see Figure 2.25). It is also released from the adrenal gland (Figure 2.3) and circulates around the body in the bloodstream, having effects at such sites as the heart. In this capacity, it acts as a hormone.

The nervous and endocrine systems interact: events within regions of the brain affect the release of certain hormones throughout the body and, reciprocally, certain hormones act on neurons. This interaction is exemplified in the next two sections.

2.5.2 Testosterone

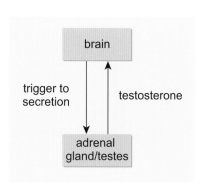

Figure 2.30 Testosterone and the brain.

The hormone **testosterone** is released from the adrenal gland in both sexes and in relatively large amounts from the testes in men. It is transported in the blood to all regions of the body (including the brain), where it exerts various effects. For example, in both sexes, testosterone acts on neurons in those brain regions that underlie the reaction to erotic stimuli and the sensitivity to erotic thoughts (Bancroft and Wu, 1983). This exemplifies a direction of cause and effect from the endocrine system to the nervous system (Figure 2.30).

There can be a reduction in the secretion of testosterone, as in surgical removal of the testes for cancer. This usually results in a fall in sexual desire. In women, loss of testosterone following surgical removal of the adrenal glands is also associated with lowering of desire. These effects exemplify the relevance of a *biopsychosocial* perspective. A medical intervention that lowers testosterone is a *biological* event but this is manifested by (amongst other effects) the *psychological* event of loss of desire (see Figure 1.8b to relate this to a biopsychosocial perspective). In turn, loss of desire might well trigger alterations in *social* behaviour.

Considering the reciprocal direction of action (i.e. from nervous system to endocrine system), the secretion of testosterone is under the influence of the brain, though not in a way open to conscious control. Furthermore, psychological factors such as stress can lower the secretion rate.

A medical intervention might also have *direct* psychological effects, in addition to those mediated by the loss of hormone. The patient will typically have insight into what is happening and make an interpretation, accompanied by expectations of what is the probable outcome. This might influence the outcome.

The discussion now turns to another example of interaction between the nervous and endocrine systems and one that enables sense to be made of earlier discussion in Chapter 1 and the present chapter.

2.5.3 Fight, flight or relaxation

Basic principles

Jim suffered a massive heart attack and it was assumed that his emotional state and behaviour had much to do with this (Chapter 1). How can emotions influence what happens at the heart?

Imagine yourself to have just confronted an angry bear in a forest. You turn and run at high speed for the nearest protection. Your heart is pumping furiously and at a high rate. The muscles of your legs are consuming a high level of nutrients and oxygen, supplied by the blood. Various nutrient substances, including fats, are released ('mobilised') into the blood for use as fuel. All these internal changes happen unconsciously and very rapidly, triggered by activity in the brain.

It is easy to appreciate the advantage to survival of being equipped with processes for mobilising resources and getting both body and behaviour into action very rapidly. This is an example of the 'fight or flight' reaction, specifically the 'flight' part of it. Of course, you could have stayed to try your luck with the fight option, in which case mobilisation of resources might appear to be equally appropriate! Assuming that you reach safety, your body will return to a more calm state with heart rate at a lower level.

Imagine now a very different situation: you are far away from forests and bears, deep in a state of meditation. Your heart rate is at a relatively low value. The low activity level of the inside of your body is appropriate to the lack of strenuous demand. Whether running from bears or meditating, the body automatically adjusts its levels of activity appropriate to the circumstances.

Returning now to Jim and his work, he exerts minimal physical effort – rather, he sits in front of a computer screen all day, putting on weight and getting ever more agitated by the perceived incompetence of his colleagues. With high blood pressure, Jim's body is acting almost as if he has just confronted a bear and yet this mobilisation of resources is quite inappropriate, since in reality Jim neither flees nor fights physically. Blood vessels (including those in the heart) get clogged up with fatty substances and the heart rate is regularly being accelerated. To understand how this happens, it is necessary to introduce another branch of the nervous system.

The autonomic nervous system

A part of the nervous system is termed the **autonomic nervous system**, abbreviated as **ANS**. It controls a range of the internal activities of the body, sometimes described as 'housekeeping functions', such as the activity of the heart and digestive system. Running from a bear and Jim's behaviour are both associated with heightened activity of a branch of the ANS.

The word 'autonomic' refers to the fact that this part of the nervous system carries on its activity *autonomously* in the absence of any control by conscious decision-making. It is extremely difficult, if not impossible, to will your heart to slow down. You can will yourself to engage in activities such as resting or meditation that might well have the effect of lowering heart rate, just as you can will yourself to run, which will accelerate it. However, these are one stage removed from directly controlling the heart itself.

Figure 2.31 shows a diagram of part of the nervous system involved in activating the leg muscles, as when running (neurons 1 and 2). It also shows part of the ANS: the neurons that convey signals to the heart (neurons 3, 4 and 5). Through such neurons as 3, 4 and 5, the ANS exerts coordinated control over the activity of the organs. When you run from a bear, your heart rate increases. This is partly the result of increased activity by the neurons of the ANS that project to the heart. As a result of activity in the ANS, the adrenal gland increases secretion of the hormones adrenalin and noradrenalin into the bloodstream. These have effects throughout the body, including reinforcing the action of the nervous system on the heart.

Conversely, as a result of activity in the ANS, blood is diverted away from the gut and there is a slowing down in the digestion of food. Digestion can be put on hold, since there are more pressing matters. Blood is needed in the muscles controlling the legs, so that you can exert the maximum effort. When you relax, blood will be automatically diverted back to the gut in relatively large amounts to facilitate digestion.

> Cardiac means pertaining to the heart. Cardiac muscle produces the beats of the heart.

■   In terms of the ANS, how would you describe Jim's problem?

☐   Jim's lifestyle was inappropriately and repeatedly triggering that part of the ANS that reacts to emergencies.

Activity 2.3 Neurotransmitters, hormones and interventions

(LOs 2.2, 2.4, 2.5 and 2.6) Allow 40 minutes

Now is the time to view the sequence 'Neurotransmitters, hormones and interventions' on the multimedia map. There are interactive exercises that will enable you to understand ways in which the activity of the nervous system can be altered and also to distinguish what are the similarities and the differences between neurotransmitters and hormones.

2.6 Final word

The emphasis of this chapter has been on ('objective') biological evidence. However, it has not lost sight of the argument developed in Chapter 1 that further understanding can be gained by a parallel consideration of subjective evidence. At this point something might be puzzling you, along the following lines.

In Chapters 1 and 2, it was noted that biological events in the brain are associated with mental events. For example, changing the activity of neurons in particular brain regions is associated with lifting Mary's and Neha's despair. Changing testosterone level is associated with changing levels of erotic desire.

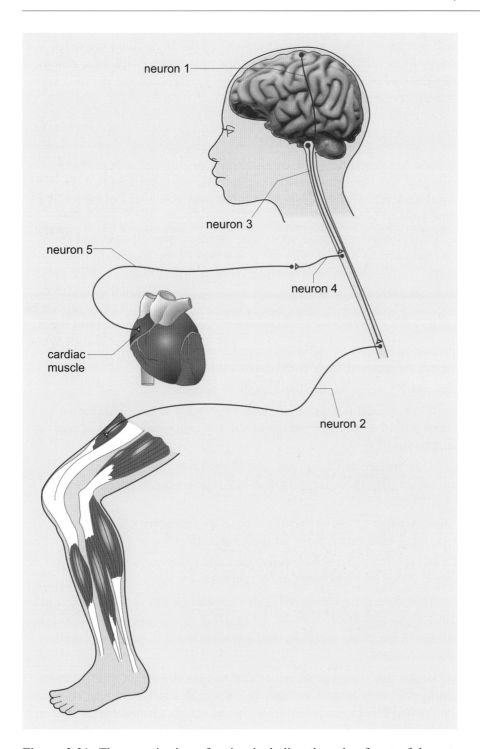

Figure 2.31 The organisation of action including the role of part of the autonomic nervous system.

You might be wondering: how can changes in the activity of neurons be associated with changes in mental states? How can something objective such as action potentials link to something subjective, such as a feeling of depression or joy? Alas, no one knows and you might regard this as something of a flaw at the basis of biological treatments of mental states.

What will be demonstrated to you throughout SDK228 are both the value and limitations of biological approaches. Thus the next chapter will look at some further examples linking biological and mental events from the point of view of examining mental well-being.

2.7 Summary of Chapter 2

- The body can be classified in various ways, one of which is in terms of organs (e.g. the brain) and another is in terms of its systems (e.g. the nervous system). All the organs of the body are composed of billions of minute cells.

- The nervous system is made up of the central nervous system and the peripheral nervous system. The brain is a part of the central nervous system. The nervous system is made up of billions of cells, a principal kind being neurons.

- Endocrine glands secrete hormones, some of which affect mood and behaviour.

- In certain techniques of neuroimaging, activity of regions throughout the brain can be inferred from blood flows to these regions.

- Under some conditions, the brain exhibits plasticity.

- An action potential is a pulse of electricity within a neuron. Information is encoded within neurons by means of the frequency with which action potentials occur.

- Signals are transmitted from one neuron to another by means of neurotransmitter. There is a lock-and-key relationship between a neurotransmitter and its receptors.

- At some synapses, neurotransmitters have an excitatory effect, whereas, at others, neurotransmitters have an inhibitory effect.

- After occupation of receptors, neurotransmitter is rapidly removed from the synapse, either by breakdown or by reuptake.

- Drugs that change psychological states act on neurons in the brain. A class of such drugs is termed 'selective serotonin reuptake inhibitors' (SSRIs).

- Some drugs act at the receptors that are normally occupied by natural neurotransmitters.

- A substance that occupies receptors and mimics the action of a natural neurotransmitter is termed an 'agonist', whereas a substance that occupies receptors and blocks the action of a natural neurotransmitter is termed an 'antagonist'.

- The nervous and endocrine systems interact. The autonomic nervous system is a part of the nervous system that controls certain internal activities of the body. In an emergency, the ANS increases the release of hormones from the adrenal gland, accelerates the heart rate and slows digestion.

2.8 Learning outcomes

LO 2.1 Describe the relevance of the nervous and endocrine systems to understanding mental health and ill-health. (KU1, KU2)

LO 2.2 Explain how information is transmitted within the nervous system by means of action potentials and neurotransmission. (KU2, KS2)

LO 2.3 Explain the relevance of abnormalities in such transmission for understanding mental ill-health. (KU2, KS2)

LO 2.4 Explain the relevance of the study of the brain to understanding mental health and ill-health. (KU4, KS1)

LO 2.5 Give some examples of where brain activity established by neuroimaging can be linked to psychological states. (KU4, KS1)

LO 2.6 Give the rationale for the use of neurochemical interventions to treat mental ill-health. (KU4, CS1)

LO 2.7 Distinguish between neuronal and hormonal transmission of information, giving examples of two-way neuronal–endocrine interaction. (KU2, CS2)

LO 2.8 Describe the relevance to health of the links between the nervous and endocrine systems. (KU2, KU3)

2.9 Self-assessment questions

SAQ 2.1 (LO 2.7)

What is meant by stating that the relationship between the nervous and endocrine systems is 'reciprocal'?

SAQ 2.2 (LO 2.4 and 2.5)

Suppose that a person with a social phobia is slowly exposed to the feared object such that their subjectively expressed fear declines. What objective measure of the decline in fear might be expected to accompany this?

SAQ 2.3 (LO 2.2)

Select one of the following to complete the sentence:

Information is communicated along the length of a neuron by means of changes in the ……… of action potentials.

(a) size

(b) length

(c) frequency

(d) shape

(e) any of (a)–(d).

SAQ 2.4 (LOs 2.2, 2.3 and 2.6)

Figure 2.32 shows activity at a synapse and the activity in the associated neurons.

(a) Is the synapse inhibitory or excitatory?

(b) Is the substance injected an agonist or antagonist to the natural neurotransmitter?

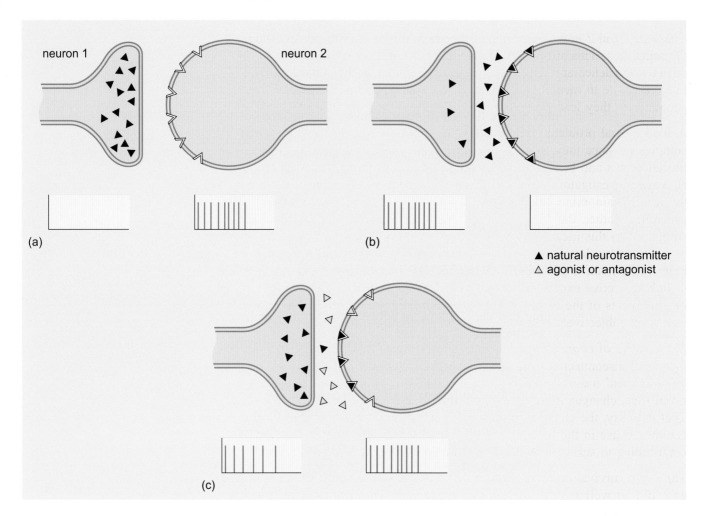

Figure 2.32 The action of a substance at synapse: (a) and (b) under two different natural conditions; (c) after appearance of an agonist or antagonist.

SAQ 2.5 (LO 2.8)

What is the logic for Jim receiving the prescription of meditation and instructions to challenge his hostile thoughts?

Chapter 3 Factors that contribute to mental well-being

Frederick Toates

3.1 Introduction

Chapters 1 and 2 argued that mental events and brain events are two sides of the same coin. This suggests a parallel consideration of subjective and objective evidence and the present chapter does this in the context of factors that contribute to mental well-being. It looks at aspects of the mental lives of people, how they lead their day-to-day lives and their social context.

A fundamental problem with investigating brain and mind arises from their complexity, since they work as one integrated whole. Subjectively reported mental events and behaviour are the product of the *whole brain and mind*. However, investigators cannot, of course, consider all the events throughout the whole brain–mind simultaneously, since this task is beyond human capability. Rather, they can only look at simplified aspects of the complex whole. Often this means observing changes over a period of time in the levels of one or a few hormones or neurotransmitters or in electrical activity of the brain as a person is placed in an experimental situation. Attempts can be made to link subjective experience to observed biological events. For example, measurements of the levels of hormones can be made before and after people engage in subjectively pleasant events (e.g. stroking a pet).

The concept of *coordination* can help you to organise what might seem to be numerous disconnected facts into a meaningful picture. The word 'coordination' means acting towards a common endpoint. For example, at a given time, changes in the body's physiology are *coordinated* with behaviour. That is to say, the changes in physiology and behaviour (a) are linked to a common cause in the brain and (b) act in the same direction: for instance, in contributing to survival. A familiar example can illustrate this.

Threats to survival come in such forms as dangerous animals, excesses of heat and cold, as well as other stimuli that cause pain. They are associated with 'negative emotions', meaning those of the kind that we try to eliminate or at least minimise. Challenges to survival, as in confronting a bear in the forest, immediately trigger a state of brain–mind that is called fear. In turn, fear triggers:

- the behaviour of fleeing
- increased activity by the autonomic nervous system (ANS) (Chapter 2).

■ How does this illustrate coordination?

□ The change in the *physiology* (e.g. elevated heart rate) helps the *behaviour* of fleeing or fighting. Changes in behaviour and physiology arise from the emotion of fear.

These days in industrialised societies, the stressful unresolved problem often does not arise from a direct physical threat to the body, such as a fire, a flood or a prowling bear. It is more likely that some sophisticated cognition is first needed in the evaluation of any threat: for example, that posed by an over-zealous tax inspector or a looming assignment deadline. Humans are exquisitely good at endlessly worrying about such problems.

Positive emotions and restraint on negative emotions are associated with good health and subjective well-being (Huppert et al., 2005). Conversely, negative emotions such as fear and anger are associated with low subjective well-being. Different emotions are characterised by particular profiles of neurotransmitter activity in the brain. These brain events trigger changes in the brain and in the body outside the brain, such as elevated levels of certain hormones in the blood and accelerated beating of the heart.

The chapter tries to unravel some of the links between cognitions, emotions and events throughout the body that are relevant to health. First though, it is necessary to return to some basics of Chapter 2 and place refinements on them, as follows in the next section.

3.2 Coordination between the nervous and endocrine systems

This chapter will be concerned with negative emotions (e.g. fear) and also positive emotions (e.g. joy). The links between these emotions and the ANS will be described. So far, the ANS has been presented in simplified terms, as if it acts as a single entity. This section will refine that description.

3.2.1 Threats and negative emotions

When a threat appears, the brain makes a decision: to fight, flee or freeze. (Of course, in modern society the decision might well be to call the police but the concern here is with the basic processes.) In coordination with behaviour, the ANS adjusts physiology. This section looks at this coordination and introduces an additional system that is involved in the reaction to threats.

Brain processes

A decision to fight or flee is associated with changes in the levels of a number of neurochemicals in the brain. One of these is *noradrenalin* and it is released at a relatively high rate at such times. Figure 3.1a shows a widely branching pathway of neurons in the brain that utilise noradrenalin as their neurotransmitter. When these neurons are active, extensive regions of the brain are put in a state appropriate for alertness and behaviour is primed for action. The brain simultaneously organises behaviour and causes changes within the ANS (see arrow to heart and adrenal gland, etc.), as summarised in Figure 3.1b.

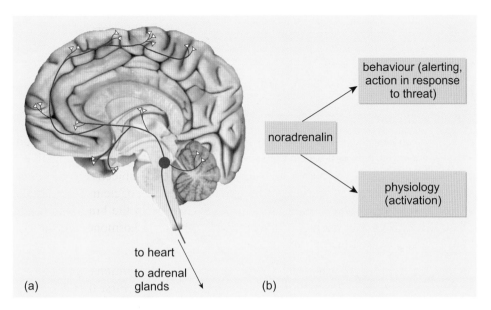

Figure 3.1 Noradrenalin: (a) pathway of neurons in the brain that utilise it; (b) coordination of its effects.

The sympathetic branch of the ANS

In reality, the ANS has two distinct branches (Figure 3.2). More specifically, negative emotions associated with the perception of threat and the decision to take action (e.g. to flee) are associated with activation of the **sympathetic branch** of the ANS. In response to increased activity in the neurons of the sympathetic branch, the body is prepared for the exertion of effort, e.g. the heart beat is accelerated and the heart pumps with greater strength.

The second branch of ANS is described in Section 3.2.3.

Considering the neurochemicals involved in the reaction to threat, coordination is evident. Noradrenalin has a role both in the control of behaviour in response to a threat and in adjusting physiology. Neurons release noradrenalin at various organs in the body, triggering them into altered action. For example, noradrenalin release occurs at junctions with cardiac muscle cells and when the noradrenalin receptors become occupied, the heart beats with greater strength and frequency.

Figure 3.3 shows the coordinated role of noradrenalin. Activity within the sympathetic branch of the ANS causes noradrenalin and adrenalin to be released from the adrenal gland. These hormones circulate in the bloodstream and affect a range of organs. On occupying receptors at the heart, they increase the vigour of its activity. Thereby, they reinforce the action of noradrenalin released as a neurotransmitter from neurons with terminals at the heart. In summary, noradrenalin acts in a *coordinated* way (Figure 3.3) as:

1 a neurotransmitter released by the neurons in the brain that are involved in organising the alerting associated with fighting or fleeing

2 the neurotransmitter released at the terminals of neurons of the sympathetic branch of the ANS

3 a hormone released from the adrenal gland.

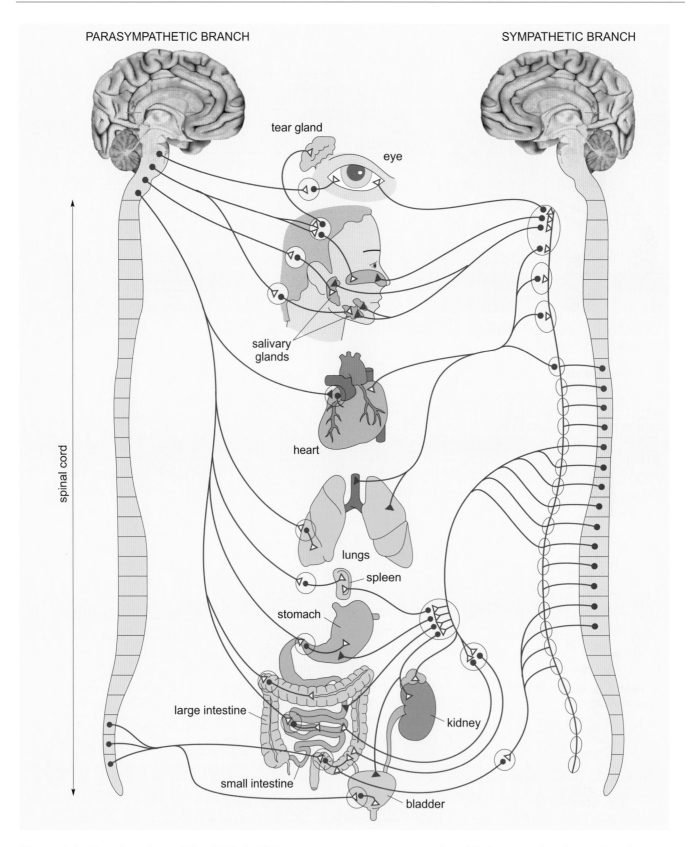

Figure 3.2 Two branches of the ANS. Inhibitory synapses are represented as filled green triangles and excitatory synapses as unfilled green triangles.

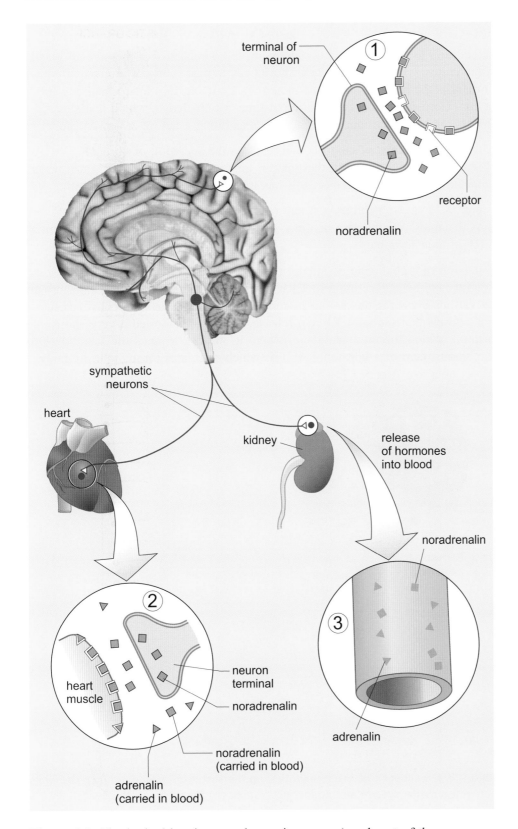

Figure 3.3 The brain (showing noradrenergic neurons) and part of the sympathetic branch of the ANS.

A parallel system of defence against threats

In addition to adrenalin and noradrenalin, the outer layer of the adrenal gland – the cortex – secretes a group of hormones termed 'corticosteroids', of which cortisol is the best–known. Corticosteroids also help to prepare the body for action. Cortisol release is increased at times of challenge, which includes threats but also such innocuous activities as doing a taxing crossword puzzle.

There is a sequence of controls that leads to the secretion of cortisol (Figure 3.4). Understanding the links in this sequence is valuable since, when something gets out of balance, this has implications for mental ill-health.

Figure 3.4a shows neurons just below a brain region known as the hypothalamus. When these neurons are active, they secrete a hormone termed **CRF** at their terminals.

CRF is an abbreviation of 'corticotropin releasing factor'.

Detection of a challenge, if intense enough, can excite activity in these neurons and hence secretion of CRF. The perception of challenge is performed by various brain regions acting in combination and signals are conveyed to the neurons that secrete CRF. On release, CRF is transported a very short distance within the pituitary gland, where it, in turn, triggers the secretion into the bloodstream of a hormone, ACTH, which circulates throughout the body.

ACTH stands for adrenocorticotropic hormone.

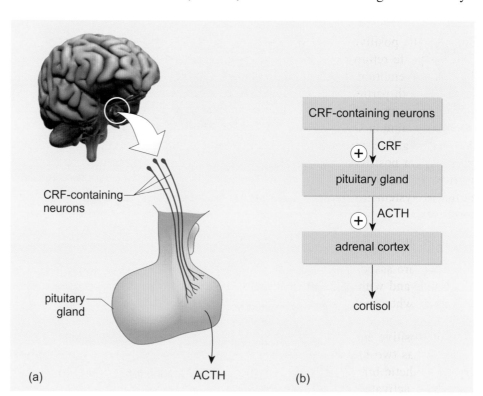

Figure 3.4 Sequence of events involved in the secretion of cortisol. (a) The links between nervous system and endocrine system. (b) Summary of the events.

Some ACTH gets to the adrenal cortex, where it triggers the release of cortisol.

Cortisol release can be something of a double-edged sword. When activated over a short period of time, it prepares the body for action. However, if the level of cortisol remains elevated for a long period, this means a failure to resolve the initial problem and represents an unhealthy state. Excessive cortisol can be damaging ('toxic') to brain tissue (Uno et al., 1989). Healthy ('appropriate') activation consists of a rise in the blood level of cortisol on confrontation with a challenge, followed by a drop in level with its resolution.

As a point of comparison, it was noted in Section 2.5.3 that the ANS can be triggered 'appropriately' in dealing with an emergency that demands physical exertion. However, it can also be triggered excessively ('inappropriately') in response to the 'minor' and repeated irritations of daily life. A similar logic can be applied to cortisol release. Cognitive challenges in trying to control a situation, as in meeting a deadline, can trigger excessive cortisol secretion (reviewed in Toates, 1995).

However, life is not all doom and gloom. In addition to emergency ('stress') systems, there are also positive emotions, associated with those parts of the neural and endocrine systems characterised as 'anti-stress', to which the chapter now turns.

3.2.2 Certain positive emotions and 'anti-stress'

Consider the positive emotions associated with parents' reaction to their children's safe return home or the greeting of a long-lost friend. Think also of the positive emotion within the human–pet bond, often experienced, it would seem, by both parties. Whereas negative emotions move us to eliminate or get *away from* aversive situations, positive emotions move us to *approach* – to form and maintain social bonds with other living beings (Post, 2007). Whereas negative emotions excite activity within the body (e.g. elevated heart rate), certain positive emotions tend to play a role in calming (e.g. lowering heart rate). Positive emotions have their own distinct biological bases in particular systems of neurons of the brain and associated neurochemicals and hormones.

■ In what way do such positive emotions illustrate coordination?

□ They are associated with both calm behaviours such as building social bonds and with calming of the physiology of the body. They arise at times when there is not a demand for large exertion.

How do positive emotions exert this effect on physiology? It was noted that the ANS has two branches with different actions. So far, you have met only the sympathetic branch. The other branch, termed the **parasympathetic branch**, is activated at times of relaxation (Figure 3.5). It releases acetylcholine at the terminals of neurons. Whereas increased activity in the sympathetic branch increases the heart rate, increased activity within the parasympathetic branch decreases it. In other words, there is a kind of tug-of-war between these two systems. The parasympathetic branch is triggered by the perception that there is a lack of threat. Activation of the system of positive emotion and the parasympathetic branch of the ANS causes inhibition

A neuron that releases acetylcholine is termed 'cholinergic'.

of the sympathetic branch and the system underlying release of cortisol, another example of coordination.

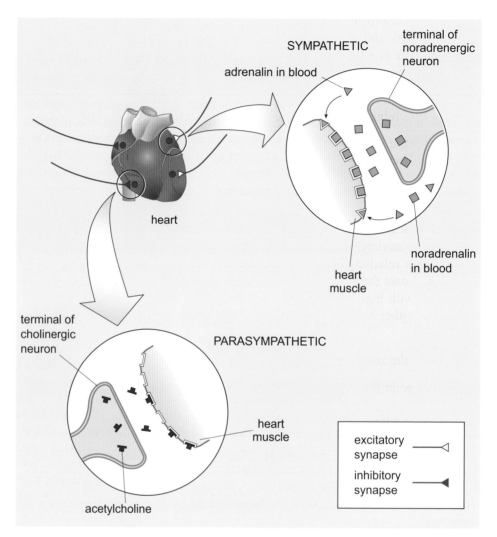

Figure 3.5 Parts of the sympathetic and parasympathetic branches of the ANS that control the activity of the heart.

The following sections deal with a series of behavioural phenomena: for example, exercise trust, altruism and meditation. An understanding of their relevance to health will call upon information on the interactions between nervous and endocrine systems just described.

3.3 Physical exercise, the nervous system and mood

Physical exercise that strongly accelerates the heart rate has various effects upon the body. This section considers the effects on brain and mind, such as the alteration of psychological states.

3.3.1 The effect on mood

Physical exercise is believed to be good for general bodily and psychological health. Evidence suggests that it lowers stress, pain and anxiety and eases depression (Otto et al., 2007). To prove that there is a beneficial role of exercise, it is not sufficient to observe that people who exercise show fewer signs of psychological disturbance than do inactive people.

■   How else might this observation be interpreted?

☐   That people with psychological disturbance tend to avoid exercise, whereas psychologically healthy people engage in it.

However, experimental evidence does show an effect of exercise on psychological condition. Participants diagnosed with mild depression or anxiety, who were prescribed exercise, showed improvements relative to the control group (Otto et al., 2007). Figure 3.6 shows the result of an experiment in which participants with high anxiety sensitivity were randomly allocated to either an exercise group or a control group (Smits et al., 2008).

■   What is the result of taking exercise?

☐   A decline in the level of both anxiety and depression.

Long-distance runners describe a 'runner's high': an elevated mood ('euphoria') that arises after considerable exertion (Boecker et al., 2008). Such terms as 'drug-like' and 'inner harmony' are also used. How does this arise and could it give clues as to the beneficial effects of exercise on mental health?

3.3.2 The biological bases of the effect on mood

There are a number of changes in the brain that occur with exercise and one or more of these could be implicated in the mood change. For example, studies in non-humans show increased activity in neurons in the brain that release serotonin and noradrenalin (Dishman, 1997). These neurochemicals form the target for various types of antidepressants (Section 2.4.1), so exercise might act somewhat like an antidepressant drug in boosting their levels but without undesirable side effects. Another neurochemical has attracted much interest, as described now.

The **endorphin hypothesis** suggests that elevated levels of neurochemicals termed endorphins in the brain form the basis of the effect on mood (Morgan, 1985). The assumption underlying the endorphin hypothesis is shown in Figure 3.7. Part (a) represents the situation prior to running and part (b) after an hour or so of running. Increased frequency of action potentials causing increased release of endorphins is associated with increased

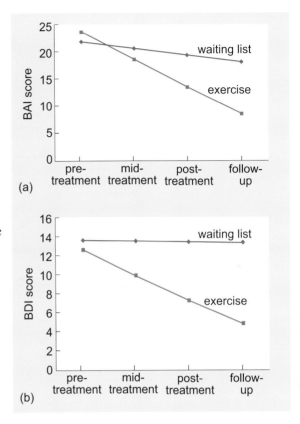

Figure 3.6 A comparison of the effects of exercise and a control condition ('waiting list'). [The control group ('waiting list') were told that they needed to wait in order to participate in the programme but were assessed at the same intervals of time as the exercise group.] (a) The measure of anxiety is the Beck Anxiety Inventory (BAI), a self-report of how the individuals feel in answer to a number of questions about the last week (e.g. how intense have been feelings of dread?). (b) The Beck Depression Inventory (BDI) is similarly a self-assessment of the intensity of sadness felt in the last week.

occupation of their receptors. Four pieces of evidence support the endorphin hypothesis:

1 Levels of endorphins in the blood increase following strenuous exercise.

2 Endorphins act as neurotransmitters in the brain.

3 Endorphins bear a close chemical similarity to opiates, such as heroin, which are associated with elevated mood when injected by users (Chapters 1 and 2).

4 In extreme cases, exercise can become addictive (Book 3, Chapter 1), which is compatible with an involvement of the opiate-like endorphins.

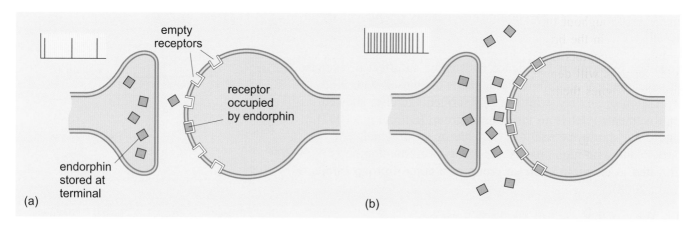

Figure 3.7 Assumption underlying the endorphin hypothesis.

The experimental manipulation of endorphin activity could be an appropriate means of gaining insight into the relationship between exercise, endorphins and mood.

You might wish to remind yourself of the meaning of the terms 'agonist' and 'antagonist' from Section 2.4.2.

■ Suppose that an antagonist to endorphins were to be injected prior to exercise. On the basis of the hypothesis, what effect would this be expected to have on the mood of the exerciser?

□ Either to eliminate or, at least, to reduce the intensity of the high that is normally experienced.

This is indeed found to be the case (Janal et al., 1984).

So far, much experimental evidence supports the endorphin hypothesis. However, further evidence is needed to complete the picture, for the following reason. Consider the two observations:

• strenuous activity is associated with increased levels of endorphins in the blood

• endorphins are found in the brain.

The pituitary gland is shown in Figures 2.3 and 3.4a.

This does not prove that increased release *in the brain* is at the basis of the effect of exercise on mood. Endorphins are also released from the pituitary gland into the bloodstream, where they are transported to distant sites. Given that moods are associated with brain states, it would be useful to get direct evidence that elevated levels of endorphins *specifically in the brain* form the basis of the effect on mood.

But how are researchers able to measure levels of occupation of endorphin receptors in the brain?

The technique of neuroimaging was described in Section 2.2.2, in terms of getting a measure of the flow of blood to different regions of the brain. There is a variation on this method that allows the detection of the amount of a selected neurochemical present at receptors in particular brain regions. Suppose that an artificial form of endorphin is *tagged* (radioactively labelled) so that its presence in the brain is identifiable. It is injected into the blood and disperses throughout the body, where it attaches to endorphin receptors, some of which are in the brain. The extent to which it does so will depend upon the number of receptors free to be occupied (Figure 3.8). In turn, the number of free receptors will depend upon the amount of the natural substance that already occupies them.

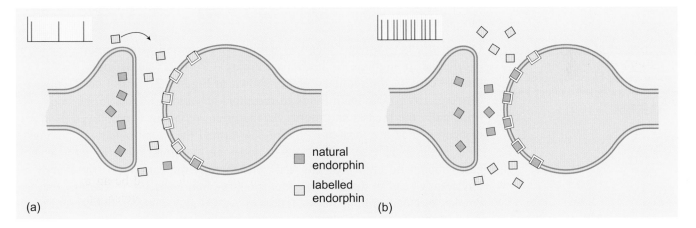

natural endorphin

labelled endorphin

(a) (b)

Figure 3.8 Technique of radioactive labelling. (a) High occupation of receptors by labelled substance. (b) Low occupation of receptors by labelled substance.

■ From Figure 3.8, what is the relationship between the amount of natural neurochemical that occupies receptors and the amount of radioactively labelled substance that does so?

☐ The more that the natural substance occupies receptors, the lower is the occupation by the labelled substance.

Hence, researchers can gain a measure of endorphin activity in brain regions (Boecker et al., 2008). The higher the report of euphoria by the runner, the higher was the calculated level of occupation of receptors by the natural endorphin, measured after euphoria was reported. Increased levels of endorphins were seen particularly in regions of the prefrontal cortex known to be implicated in emotional processing (Section 2.2.2).

The involvement of endorphins in the runner's high does not prove that they are also implicated in the effect of less strenuous exercise on mood but it suggests this possibility.

The next section will focus on another chemical that serves as both neurotransmitter and hormone and which is involved in positive emotions.

3.4 Social bonds and their effects on mental health

3.4.1 The underlying processes

Basics

In a number of species, close bonds between individuals are formed (Panksepp, 1998). Clearly, in humans, examples of social bonds include those between romantic partners, parents and their children, as well as close friends. This section considers the biological basis of such social bonds. The neurochemical termed 'oxytocin' plays a primary role in the CNS in behavioural calming and the establishment of bonds and close contact between living beings (Uvnäs-Moberg et al., 2005). Subjectively, its influence is felt as one of well-being.

Measurement of cortisol in saliva is relatively easy and does not involve taking blood samples. Saliva cortisol levels reflect levels in the blood.

Oxytocin acts as a neurochemical within the brain and as a hormone distributed throughout the body (see Figure 3.9). It is released into the bloodstream by the pituitary gland, shown in Figures 2.3 and 3.4a (Uvnäs-Moberg, 1998). Oxytocin binds to receptors at various targets in the body, principally the breasts and uterus. In the brain, oxytocin is employed by a set of neurons that are located in the region termed the 'hypothalamus', amongst other regions. This set of neurons provides an important input to activate the parasympathetic branch of the ANS, and thereby the calming of the body's physiology (e.g. in decreasing blood pressure and heart rate). Neurons that employ oxytocin inhibit the secretion of ACTH and, thereby, the secretion of cortisol (Coiro et al., 1988).

Figure 3.10 shows the result of an experiment that measured cortisol levels in the saliva of participants as they confronted a challenge (Heinrichs et al., 2003). The challenge consisted of performing public speaking followed by a mental arithmetic task in front of a panel of evaluators. Participants were divided into four groups as shown in the figure. Two groups received oxytocin via a nasal spray, whereas two groups received placebo. (The meaning of placebo is given in Section 1.2.3.) One placebo group and one oxytocin group were also allowed the social support of being in the presence of their best friend.

- ■ What do the results show?

- □ Receiving oxytocin lowers the cortisol response, as does social support. Combining the oxytocin spray with social support gives an even stronger inhibition of cortisol secretion.

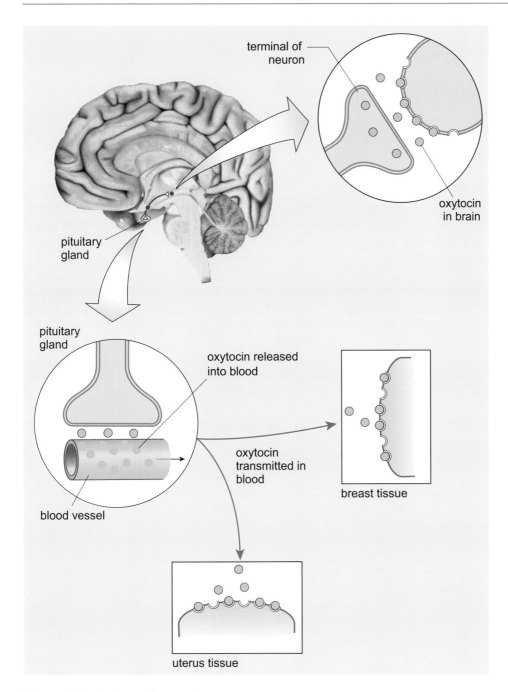

Figure 3.9 Actions of oxytocin.

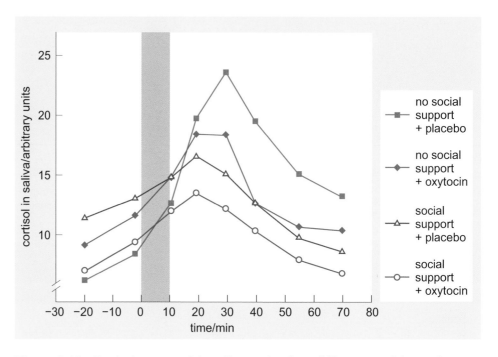

Figure 3.10 Cortisol measured in saliva under four different conditions of stress. The shaded area indicates period of the challenge.

The action of oxytocin illustrates coordination (Figure 3.11).

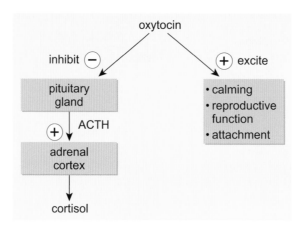

Figure 3.11 Coordination in the action of oxytocin.

One situation that triggers oxytocin release into the circulation is breastfeeding in women. In turn, oxytocin has a role in milk ejection. Breastfeeding women are calmed by oxytocin (Uvnäs-Moberg, 1998) and breastfeeding is an appropriate time for calming and bonding between mother and infant.

Within the field of psychology, there is an increasing awareness of the plasticity of the brain (Section 2.2.2) corresponding to personal experience.

Early activation of the oxytocin system might have implications for the development of features of the human nervous system and thereby behaviour. Scientific research cannot yet answer the question of how important oxytocin is in the brain of the baby for the process of developing an attachment with the mother during suckling. Uvnäs-Moberg et al. (2005, p. 63) speculate:

> It is tempting to suggest that an adequate stimulation of the calm and connection system during early life is of utmost importance for the establishment of the brain and related biological structures that can form the platform for the development of a socialised individual.

In a range of species, it has been shown that suckling is a stimulus for the release of oxytocin in the mother (Fuchs et al., 1987). However, there is a complication to this and it is revealed in the sample responses shown by women in Figure 3.12 (McNeilly et al., 1983).

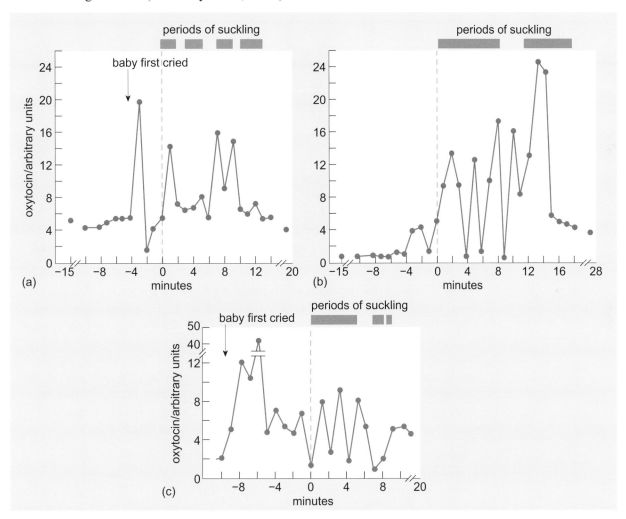

Figure 3.12 Sample responses of blood oxytocin levels in three women. The horizontal axis shows minutes relative to the start of suckling.

■   What do these results tell you about the onset of oxytocin release in relation to the start of suckling?

□   That the release of oxytocin occurs *before* suckling starts.

The authors conclude that conditioning is involved in the release of oxytocin.

Activity 3.1 Exploring conditioning

(LOs 3.1 and 3.3) Allow 15 minutes

Conditioning was introduced in Section 1.3.2. Before going on, write short notes to consider the following two related questions. If conditioning is involved in the result shown in Figure 3.12, what kind of conditioning would it be? How would such conditioning arise and how might you in principle establish that conditioning is the explanation?

3.4.2 Trust

Oxytocin has a close link to the trust that humans show (Zak et al., 2005). Activity by oxytocin in the brain increases a person's tendency to show trust. Reciprocally, when someone is shown trust, there is increased activation of oxytocin in the brain of the trusted one.

In an experimental demonstration, participants played the role of either investor or trustee (Kosfeld et al., 2005). Participants were anonymous to each other. Investors sent money to trustees, who could either invest it and share the profit with the investor or abscond with it. Participants were divided into two groups: receiving oxytocin via an intranasal spray, or receiving placebo. Each participant received 12 monetary units, which could either be kept or invested.

Figure 3.13a shows the average investment ('transfer') made by investors. Of those receiving oxytocin, 45% (0.45) invested all 12 monetary units, whereas only 21% of the control group did so. Could the effect really be one of trust or could it simply be that oxytocin makes investors less averse to risk? The experiment was repeated but instead of dealing with a human investor, there was a random investment allocation made by a computer. In this case, there was no difference between oxytocin and control groups (Figure 3.13b). In other words, oxytocin appears to influence trust when a person is dealing specifically with another human rather than with a machine.

Alas, this effect is open to commercial exploitation: oxytocin sprays are available on the internet with the suggestion that they will increase trust and thereby improve one's social and commercial success.

3.4.3 Altruism

The term **altruism** refers to a type of action that is concerned with the well-being of others rather than oneself (Post, 2007). Examples of altruism abound: for example, many people leave tips in restaurants that they are very unlikely ever to visit again or give anonymous donations to charities.

There is evidence that altruism is good for the health not only of the recipient but also the one showing altruistic behaviour (Post, 2007). A caution needs to

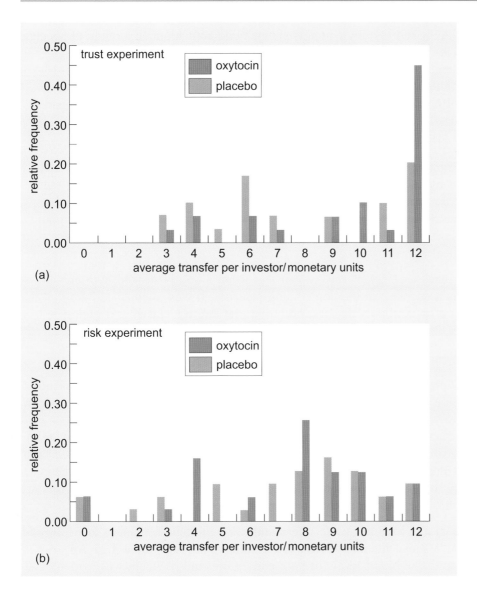

Figure 3.13 Transfer of monetary units made by investors receiving oxytocin and control groups: (a) when dealing with a human trustee; (b) when dealing with a computer making random allocations.

be stated: altruism taken to the extreme is most unlikely to be beneficial. This is expressed in the term 'burden of care'. Benefits arise only from altruism 'within reason'.

There are various ways in which altruism, as in volunteer work, might contribute to good mental health (Oman, 2007). For example, the volunteer could gain a sense of self-efficacy and being needed, with a purpose in life. The altruist might also be distracted from his or her own problems. This is the kind of evidence at a psychological level but might it also relate to a biological basis?

The opportunity to help another person counters excessive activity by the heart following exposure to a stressor (Brown et al., 2007). It appears that the positive emotion of helping provides an input to the parasympathetic branch of the ANS and thereby counters sympathetic activation. In a range of species, oxytocin is released at times of positive social contact (Marques and Sternberg, 2007; Uvnäs-Moberg et al., 2005). It reduces anxiety, increases social interaction and decreases the stress reaction of the body (e.g. it lowers cortisol levels). Oxytocin is a strong candidate for a prime role in altruism.

3.4.4 Interactions between humans and pets

It is commonly argued that companion animals bring health benefits to their owners by such means as reducing loneliness and alienation, by giving the owner a purpose in life and some control over their environment. Of course, particularly in the case of dog owners, the pet is said to offer unconditional love! Is it possible to link any of these psychological phenomena to their biological bases?

As far back as 1929, it was known that when a dog is stroked by a human, there is a decrease in the dog's blood pressure. It was established later that the human also exhibits a decrease in blood pressure (Odendaal and Meintjes, 2003; Dizon et al., 2007).

■   What does this suggest regarding the control of the ANS?

□   There is a shift in relative level of activity from the sympathetic to the parasympathetic branch in dog and human alike.

Since many people find stroking cats and dogs to be irresistible, this suggests the possibility of a chemical change triggered by such contact and which both affects the control of the heart and serves to *reinforce* (Section 1.3.2) the activity of stroking. Furthermore, being in the presence of one's pet lowers both objective and subjective measures of stress (Dizon et al., 2007).

Odendaal and Meintjes (2003) observed some biological changes that followed a positive social interaction between a human and dog (Table 3.1). An increase in the blood levels of both endorphins and oxytocin was evident. As a control condition, the same participants were asked to spend the same length of time doing quiet reading. In each case, the effect of interaction with a pet was greater in the four variables listed in Table 3.1 than the reading condition.

Table 3.1 Changes in some factors in humans over the course of a positive interaction with a dog.

The units (such as mmHg) are included for completeness only.

	Before	**After**
Arterial blood pressure (mmHg)	87.6	84.4
Oxytocin in blood (ng 1^{-1})	2.1	4.0
β-endorphin in blood (pmol 1^{-1})	3.1	8.0
Cortisol in blood (mmol 1^{-1})	317.0	309.0

These results suggest a value of animals in therapy for people who have suffered stressful experiences.

This study used the same participants under both conditions of the experiment and is known as a within-participants design (Box 3.1).

Box 3.1 Research Methods: Within- or between-participants designs

Section 3.4.4 describes an experiment in which various physiological changes are measured after interaction with a pet and compared to the same changes measured after a period of quiet reading. In this study, the same participants appeared in both the experimental and control conditions. It is therefore termed a **within-participants design**, meaning that the comparisons are made of data obtained from the same participants. This is in contrast to the study described in Box 2.2, which was a between-participants design. Between-participants designs compare data obtained from different participants. At the stage of designing an experiment, the researchers need to decide which of these two designs they will employ. There are several factors that would influence this decision.

Availability of participants

For a within-participants design, since participants take part in both conditions, only half as many of them are needed as for between-participants designs. If participants are in short supply, this can bias towards a within-participants design. However, of course, each participant needs to spend twice as long under observation as for a between-participants design.

Problems of matching

As mentioned in Box 2.2, some between-participants designs use matched participants to reduce the problems of variation between individuals. It is, however, difficult to match all human characteristics, or indeed to decide which characteristics should be matched. There will inevitably be some individual differences between participants in the two conditions. For a within-participants design, each participant is, of course, perfectly matched with himself or herself. Hence, there is no problem of trying to make sure that there is balance in participants in the two conditions. The possibility of individual differences interfering with the results of the study is eliminated.

Order effects

Within-participants designs may be preferable in principle, but there is a danger that what is termed an **order effect** can arise. Suppose that, in the pet study, all of the participants were tested in the order: (1) quiet reading, (2) interaction with a pet. Suppose further that they were rather concerned at the prospect of being involved in scientific research but after taking part in the quiet reading condition their fears were allayed. They would then enter the experimental condition of interacting with a pet as changed people compared to the start of the experiment. It may be that in the second condition the reduction in blood pressure is enhanced due to the previous experience of taking part in the first condition. Hence, any apparent effect of interacting with the pet would be due in part to this factor rather than the pet. Conversely, some national event of great significance such as a terrorist attack might have taken place just prior to condition 2 being tested and this could cause an elevated blood pressure and therefore mask the effect of the interaction with a pet. To counter the possibility of such order effects, participants must be randomly allocated to two groups, where half of the participants are tested in the order (1) → (2) and the other half in the order (2) → (1). Random allocation to order of conditions does not eliminate the sorts of effects described above, but it ensures that they appear equally in the two conditions and therefore will not produce spurious results.

Predefined participants

In some studies, the participants in the two conditions have to be different: for example, investigations of differences between men and women, people of different ages or people with and without a health condition. In these cases, there is no option but to have a between-participants design.

The next section looks at another class of events in the brain–mind and its relevance to well-being.

3.5 Cognition, attention and well-being

Activity 3.2 Reflecting on thinking
(LO 3.3) Allow 5 minutes

Take a moment to reflect on your thought processes, the stream of consciousness that you experience now and in the past. Jot down a few notes on the contents of the thoughts and whether you appear to be in control of them.

This section briefly considers the nature of attention and cognition and their implications for health and subjective well-being. Trying to link a person's mental state to their physical health is a daunting task and some of the associated methodological problems are described more fully in Chapter 4. This section will simply introduce some of the bases of the evidence.

3.5.1 Meditation

There are various techniques of meditation. Their devotees tend to use an esoteric language (e.g. 'pure consciousness') to describe the effects, which does not easily map onto a more scientifically based account. However, from an outsider's perspective, the techniques appear to have in common that they are means to attain a subjective experience of 'blissful awareness' (Jevning et al., 1992). To do this, they seek to *regulate* the process of attention in mental life. Often the skill of focusing attention upon only a desired thought or object, in the face of distractions, is being sought (Lutz et al., 2008). Some techniques involve a focus on the pattern of breathing.

The specific technique termed 'transcendental meditation' (TM) has attracted the most scientific research and consists of repeating a particular word called a 'mantra' in the mind for two 20-minute periods each day. By means of this voluntary focus of attention, meditation is said to benefit the state of consciousness (Orme-Johnson et al., 2006). It is claimed to lower stress and anxiety, as well as to reduce pain.

Meditation is associated with reduced heart and breathing rates, apparently arising from increased activity by the parasympathetic branch of the ANS. With long-term practice, cortisol levels are reduced (Jevning et al., 1992; Newberg and Iversen, 2003). Exactly what occurs in the brain in meditation is still somewhat speculative, so no more than tentative pointers can be given. Parts of the brain that increase in activity during certain types of meditation include regions of the prefrontal cortex (PFC) (Newberg and Iversen, 2003). This area is known to be activated when someone is consciously focusing attention on a task and not just reacting to events in the environment. The PFC makes extensive neuronal connections to other brain regions whereby it can exert control over the activity of neurons ('transfer of information') within these regions. For example, it can adjust the activity that arises from stimuli impinging on the sense organs. As practitioners become adept at meditation (e.g. less mental effort involved), it would be expected that changes in patterns of connections between neurons in the brain would occur – an example of plasticity (Section 2.3.2).

The **Stroop task** (Figure 3.14) consists of trying to name the colour of the ink of each word, ignoring the meaning of the word. You will surely find that the task is easier for the list in part (a) compared to part (b). In part (b), word meaning interferes with colour naming. Such interference is reduced by practising meditation (Wenk-Sormaz, 2005). This suggests that meditation increases the capacity to ignore information irrelevant to the task at hand.

Several studies report an overall increase in the metabolic breakdown products ('metabolites') of serotonin in the urine following meditation (Newberg and Iversen, 2003).

The term 'metabolite' is explained in Section 2.3.2.

- ■ What does this indicate?

- □ If more serotonin is being broken down, then there must have been more released in the brain during meditation.

Serotonin is implicated in mood and its activation could contribute to the 'feel good' factor linked to meditation. However, evidence points to meditation having a wider range of effects, as described now.

Link to stress

In experienced practitioners of TM, triggers to stress are associated with a lower rise in cortisol than in controls (Jevning et al., 1992).

- ■ Does this show unambiguously the effect of TM on stress?

- □ Not without further evidence, since it could be that people who are less vulnerable to stress tend to take up TM.

	(a)		(b)
BLUE	YELLOW	YELLOW	RED
GREEN	RED	GREEN	GREEN
RED	BLUE	BLUE	YELLOW
YELLOW	GREEN	RED	GREEN
RED	RED	YELLOW	BLUE
YELLOW	YELLOW	RED	RED
GREEN	BLUE	GREEN	YELLOW
BLUE	GREEN	BLUE	RED
RED	YELLOW	YELLOW	BLUE
GREEN	BLUE	BLUE	RED
YELLOW	YELLOW	GREEN	BLUE
GREEN	GREEN	BLUE	GREEN
BLUE	RED	GREEN	RED
RED	BLUE	YELLOW	YELLOW

Figure 3.14 The Stroop task: (a) compatible condition (name of colour matches ink colour); (b) incompatible condition (name of colour different from ink colour).

However, experimentation points to a link between the practice and a lowering of reaction to stress. A group of Chinese students were trained in meditation (Tang et al., 2007). After being given a mental arithmetic test, the rise in cortisol was significantly less in those given meditation training than in controls.

Link to pain

The term 'anterior' refers to the part of the structure towards the front of the brain.

The expression 'pain matrix' refers to those regions of the brain that change their activity when a person is exposed to a painful stimulus. One region in particular, termed the anterior cingulate cortex (ACC) (Figure 3.15), underlies the emotional quality of pain.

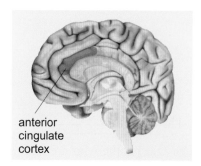

anterior
cingulate
cortex

Figure 3.15 Brain showing the anterior cingulate cortex.

Using brain neuroimaging, researchers investigated whether TM affects the brain's processing of painful stimuli (Orme-Johnson et al., 2006). So, activity of the pain matrix in response to a painful stimulus was examined in practitioners of TM (at a time outside their 20-minute meditation period), as compared to controls. The controls were then taught to practise TM and retested five months later.

The two groups did not differ in their subjective assessment of the *intensity* of the painful stimulus. However, the TM practitioners showed much lower activity in the pain matrix than did controls, particularly in the ACC. After five months of practising TM, the controls had a low activity level in the pain matrix comparable to that of the original TM practitioner group. This result corresponds to the observation that TM practitioners have the same detection of the *existence* of pain as controls but are less distressed by it. It suggests that, in processing information on pain, there is some dissociation between the awareness of a noxious trigger and the aversive emotional state that it causes.

Link to health of the circulation

In one study, meditation was prescribed for a group of African American men and women who had high blood pressure (Schneider et al., 1995). African Americans are particularly prone to hypertension, and disorders related to the circulation are much more common, on average, in this group than in white Americans. The average levels of stress experienced by African Americans are particularly high and this probably exerts a role in elevating blood pressure. It appears that high activity by the sympathetic branch of the ANS underlies the effect. This is possibly associated with overactivity in the hormonal link between CRF, ACTH and cortisol, shown in Figure 3.4b. Enormous health benefits in terms of life expectancy derive from lowering blood pressure.

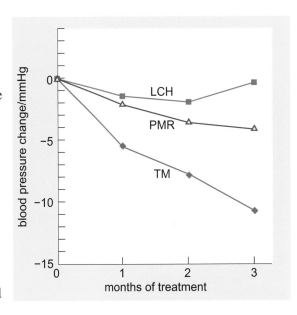

Figure 3.16 Reduction in blood pressure for TM group as compared with controls. LCH, lifestyle and circulatory health; PMR, progressive muscle relaxation; TM, transcendental meditation.

Participants were invited to practise TM for two periods of 20 minutes each day. The TM group was compared with two control groups: one was merely given directions on lifestyle and circulatory health, whereas the other was instructed in progressive muscle relaxation. The TM group experienced significant reductions in blood pressure compared to controls (Figure 3.16), indicative of a shift in the balance of activity from sympathetic to parasympathetic branches of the ANS.

3.5.2 Interacting with nature

Psychological benefits of interacting with natural environments (e.g. woods, lakes) have long been claimed. One argument is that nature specifically has a restorative effect on *directed attention* (Kaplan, 1995).

To exemplify this, think of completing an assignment. You are trying *voluntarily* ('intentionally') to bring 'directed attention' to bear on it. However, simultaneously, your attention is being drawn *involuntarily* ('automatically') to loud noises from the next room. There is conflict and maintenance of directed attention on the assignment is subjectively felt as effortful. Success requires inhibiting the effect of the attention-grabbing candidate – the loud noises. Sustained employment of directed attention leads to fatigue and, for such people as controllers of industrial machinery and airline pilots, the consequences can be catastrophic. Directed attention can be restored through interaction with nature (e.g. a lunch-time walk in the countryside).

Exactly how nature exerts this effect is still unclear but a number of experiments have demonstrated the benefits to attention of interacting with nature (Kaplan, 1995; Berman et al., 2008) (Figure 3.17). For example, proofreading (checking printed text for errors) is demanding of directed attention and it exhibits a beneficial effect of exposure to nature. Even looking at pictures of natural scenes has a restorative effect, as compared to pictures of urban scenes (Berman et al., 2008). Naturally, investigators ask what it is about nature that has this effect. Could it simply be a lack of demand for directed attention in the scenery? No: a critical piece of evidence is that exposure to a regular geometrical pattern does not have this restorative value.

The effects in terms of gaining greater control over the object of attention are similar to those reported for meditation (Kaplan, 2001). Yet, whereas meditation requires extensive effort and practice, no prerequisite skill is involved in interacting with nature. There are obviously profound implications of these findings for those responsible for designing human environments and permitting access to the countryside. There could be potential therapeutic implications for treating depression, where repetitive ('stuck in the groove') negative thinking so often predominates (Carver et al., 2008).

3.5.3 Events over periods of a lifetime

An interesting question is how *attitudes* (e.g. optimistic or pessimistic) that individuals adopt to life events might have implications for health. In therapy, not only are life events themselves considered important but so too are the ways in which they are interpreted (Gilbert and Leahy, 2009). These attitudes can be manifest in speech to others but also in silent speech, the inner dialogue that people hold with themselves. Sometimes people document in diaries how they feel about themselves and their lives and this might give signs relevant to the health that they later enjoy. This section considers some evidence on the question.

(a)

(b)

Figure 3.17 What kind of effects would such environments be expected to have?

The Harvard study

The term **explanatory style** describes how people explain to themselves unfortunate events that befall them. In one study, the explanatory style of a group of graduates from Harvard University in the period 1942–1944 was examined (Peterson et al., 1988). The Harvard researchers defined three aspects of this (Table 3.2). Take, for example, a bad assignment result and the kind of explanatory style that might be brought to it.

Table 3.2 The three aspects of different explanatory styles.

Aspect 1	
Stable	*Unstable*
This reflects my incompetence	This was a one-time aberrant event
Aspect 2	
Global	*Specific*
This will ruin all my academic career and my whole life	It is unfortunate but of no great consequence
Aspect 3	
Internal	*External*
It was my fault	It was a lousy set of questions

A person who explains the unfortunate events that befall them with stable, global and internal causes is said to have a 'pessimistic explanatory style'. Conversely, an 'optimistic explanatory style' is associated with using an unstable, specific and external explanatory style. In the Harvard study, explanatory style at age 25 was associated with differences in health status measured 30 years later. Those adopting a pessimistic explanatory style were less healthy than the optimists. Why should optimists be healthier than pessimists? Obviously, there are many factors that could be involved.

- ■ What are some of these?

- □ Pessimists might drink more alcohol to try to 'dissolve' their troubles. They might feel that there is no point in seeking medical care or adopting a healthy diet.

The Harvard researchers suggest that pessimists might be more socially isolated than optimists. As discussed in the last section, social contact appears to be an important buffer against stress. These possible factors all involve different *behaviours* by optimists and pessimists.

- ■ What other factor might be implicated?

- □ Differences in *physiological* reaction associated with differences in explanatory style.

A possibility is that placing pessimistic interpretations on life events could be associated with a greater activity of the sympathetic branch relative to the parasympathetic branch of the ANS. This could have implications for the health of, for example, the circulatory system and hence the likelihood of a stroke or heart attack. Obviously, in an 'ideal world' it would be desirable to keep as many factors as possible near to constant and just examine the factor of explanatory style in relation to physiology. In practice, clearly this is impossible. However, a study that moves nearer to this ideal is described next.

The study of nuns

How long someone lives (their 'longevity') obviously depends upon a variety of factors such as genetic inheritance, diet, smoking and alcohol consumption.

How could a researcher extract a role of *mental life* from this? The autobiographical writing of 180 Catholic nuns at age 22 years was compared with their longevity some 60 years later (Danner et al., 2001). Given the relative homogeneity of this group of subjects, they offered perhaps a unique opportunity to investigate the role of thinking style. They were all members of the School Sisters of Notre Dame and lived in the USA. The Mother Superior had made a request in 1930 that her 'flock' should write autobiographical notes.

The participants had the same, or very similar, reproductive histories, social support networks, socioeconomic status, and tobacco and alcohol intakes. Their engagement in worldly and spiritual activities was similar, as was their access to medical facilities. Those employing the largest number of positive emotion words in their autobiographical notes were found to live some 6 to 10 years longer than those using the fewest. This suggests that positive emotions exert beneficial effects on the physiology of the body.

3.6 Final word

This chapter has described the roles of several neurotransmitters and hormones: for example, that of oxytocin in bonding and calming, exemplifying the notion of coordination. It has illustrated some of the principal arguments of Chapters 1 and 2 concerning a biopsychosocial perspective and reductionism. It has reinforced the argument that a full account can only be given by considering both objective and subjective evidence. An account of meditation that looked only at such things as brain activity and hormone levels but omitted the subjective accounts of the meditator's conscious mind would be a very strange one. Similarly, an account of trust, altruism or love based upon oxytocin but omitting such psychological factors as feelings and wishes would seem impoverished. This example illustrates particularly well the need to include social context in any account.

Even when considering just the objective perspective, the role of neurotransmitters and hormones needs to be understood in terms of the organisation of the *whole system*: brain and body outside the brain. A reductionist approach indeed gains insight from studying isolated chemicals such as oxytocin but this information needs to be interpreted in a broader context.

In this light, it would be wrong to see a single chemical as a magic bullet or 'universal good news' or, alternatively, as the villain of the piece ('universal bad news'). For example, there was emphasis on the harm that can come from excessive activity by noradrenalin, in terms of blood pressure. However, it was mentioned that noradrenalin in the brain can be boosted by physical exercise with potential benefits for people suffering from depression.

3.7 Summary of Chapter 3

- Changes in biological events, such as levels of particular hormones and neurotransmitters, link to changes in subjective experience and psychological well-being.

- The notion of coordination describes changes in physiology and behaviour which can be linked to a common cause in the brain and which act together to a given end.

- There are two branches of the ANS: the sympathetic and parasympathetic.

- Noradrenalin is employed (i) as a neurotransmitter in the brain, (ii) at the terminals of neurons of the sympathetic branch of the ANS and (iii) as a hormone released by the adrenal gland. Noradrenalin is activated in a coordinated way at times of threat.

- Adrenalin is also released as a hormone from the adrenal gland.

- A system of defence against threats involves cortisol released from the adrenal gland. There is a sequence of events: [negative emotion] → [CRF] → [ACTH] → [cortisol].

- Positive emotions are the trigger to behavioural quiescence and activation of the parasympathetic branch, with inhibition of the sympathetic branch.

- Studies suggest a beneficial effect of physical exercise on mood.

- In some cases, a 'runner's high' is experienced. The endorphin hypothesis suggests that activation of endorphins within the brain forms a basis of the runner's high.

- Oxytocin plays a role in the brain in causing behavioural calming, associated with activation of the parasympathetic branch of the ANS. Oxytocin plays a role in behaviour characterised as 'trust' and appears to be implicated in altruism.

- Various factors appear to have beneficial effects on health and mental efficiency: altruistic behaviour, interaction with a pet and meditation.

- Exposure to a natural environment has beneficial effects on attention.

- Explanatory style and level of optimism/pessimism appear to have effects on health.

3.8 Learning outcomes

LO 3.1 Explain what is meant by coordination between behaviour and physiology and, by so doing, demonstrate an understanding of links between the nervous and endocrine systems. (KU1, KU2, KU3, CS1)

LO 3.2 Describe the working of the autonomic nervous system in terms of the actions of its branches. (KU1, KU2, CS1)

LO 3.3 Explain how some common activities such as keeping pets, exercise and meditation might be understood scientifically and their efficacy for mental well-being tested. (KU4, CS1, CS2, CS3, CS4)

LO 3.4 Justify the assumption that social attachment and belonging are important to good health. (KU3, CS1)

3.9 Self-assessment questions

SAQ 3.1 (LOs 3.1, 3.2 and 3.3)

The end of Section 2.5.3 described the situation of post-exercise relaxation with activation of digestion. In what way does this illustrate coordination?

SAQ 3.2 (LOs 3.1 and 3.2)

A person has an excessively high heart rate and pumping strength. Which of the following might be considered as a treatment?

(a) an agonist to noradrenalin

(b) an antagonist to noradrenalin

(c) an agonist to acetylcholine

(d) an antagonist to acetylcholine.

SAQ 3.3 (LOs 3.1 and 3.3)

Suppose that an increased level of noradrenalin in the bloodstream is associated with the runner's high. Why would it not be *sufficient* to attribute to this substance a role in producing the psychological effect?

SAQ 3.4 (LOs 3.1 and 3.4)

What is meant by claiming that the role of oxytocin exemplifies coordination between behaviour and physiology?

SAQ 3.5 (LOs 3.1 and 3.3)

(a) How might the phenomenon of meditation be related to the general assumptions concerning the relationship between brain and mind (Chapter 1)?

(b) Describe meditation in a way that involves use of the terms 'brain', 'cell', 'neuron' and 'serotonin'.

Chapter 4 Diagnosing mental illness

Antonio Martins-Mourao

4.1 Introduction

In Chapter 1 you have read about John, Neha and Angie and how they have coped with mental health issues of very different natures. You have also heard how these issues have affected their lives. John, for example, has obsessive–compulsive disorder (OCD) and spends hours scrubbing his hands in hot water and detergent. He has great trouble resisting his compulsion but thinks his behaviours can be explained by an inherited brain disorder. Neha, on the other hand, suffers from depression and has been off work for months. She feels totally alone and helpless, sees no purpose in living, and finds it difficult to get up in the morning. She wonders if there is light at the end of the tunnel after suffering the loss of both parents and the effects of a traumatic divorce. Finally, 19-year-old Angie hears voices that frighten her. She also feels isolated and unsupported by her parents, one of whom insists that she is just making up stories. Angie is upset and blames them for being bad parents and has been using cannabis to distract her mind from these problems.

People have different histories and backgrounds. They also report the feelings associated with their experiences, as well as the origins of these experiences, in different ways that help them find meaning to what is occurring to them (personal narratives, as explained in Chapter 1). So, given this variability between individuals, how can psychologists distinguish those who are only going through a 'difficult patch' in their lives from others who may actually be showing evidence of mental disorder, or abnormal behaviour? What are the processes and methods involved in the assessment and diagnosis of a person with a mental disorder, and what steps must be taken to ensure they get the best available treatment? These are the questions we will be addressing in this chapter. But first, we need to define what is meant by terms such as 'abnormality' and mental illness.

4.1.1 Defining abnormality

> If you talk to God, you are praying;
> If God talks to you, you have schizophrenia.

> (Thomas Szasz, 1973)

Although most people will probably feel sad and anxious at some point in their lives, their expression of these feelings may at times become abnormal or disordered. The question of when someone's experience of these normal emotions becomes a cause for concern is not easy to answer, especially when the term 'abnormal' can be used in a variety of ways that need not signify mental disorder. For instance it can refer to behaviour that is relatively uncommon, found only in a minority of people in a population. Rarity, of course, need not signify 'mental disorder'. Only a small minority would describe themselves as 'happy almost all the time' but they are not considered

Abnormal: something deviating from the normal, usual or expected.

to be mentally disordered. 'Abnormal' can also mean what society at a particular juncture deems 'deviant' or 'nonconformist' because it does not fit in with accepted social norms or rules of morality – a point to which we will return in Section 4.2.6, dedicated to the potential dangers of diagnosis.

'Abnormal psychology' is an umbrella term for the study of mental disorders and illness.

In mental health settings, however, the term **abnormal** is used to qualify behaviours and experiences that may indicate mental illness. **Mental illness**, on the other hand, is generally defined as a behavioural pattern that is thought to cause significant psychological suffering, distress or disability that may represent potential risk to the self or others. Mental illness usually disables the person from functioning adequately as an individual in a specified set of circumstances, such as professional environments, or in a particular role: for example, as a parent in charge of minors.

■ Which key words define mental illness?

□ Suffering, distress, disability and risk.

4.1.2 Defining diagnosis and assessment

The term diagnosis comes from the Greek *diagignoskein*, which means to distinguish or discern. In this chapter, the term **diagnosis** will refer to the process used by clinicians to determine whether a person's signs and symptoms fit a particular syndrome in a way that is causing them significant distress, disability and/or risk. Make a note of the following definitions which will be used throughout the chapter:

• A **sign** is an objective indication of mental disease that may be noticed by others, such as weeping or a slumped posture, for example.

• A **symptom** is a subjective and uncomfortable sensation that indicates a change in a person's functioning like a headache, for instance. Whereas a sign can be seen by an external observer, a symptom is usually reported by the person.

• A **syndrome**, on the other hand, is a group of symptoms and signs occurring in a specific pattern that suggests the existence of a disorder: for example, Neha's reported feelings of sadness and insomnia are some of the symptoms that form the syndrome of depression.

However, signs, symptoms and syndromes indicate a disorder only if they are thought to cause significant psychological suffering, distress or disability that may represent potential risk to the self or others.

Diagnoses are crucial for clinical practice but also for research in mental health. At the clinical level, a competent diagnosis is a prerequisite for appropriate treatment, and the failure of particular treatments may help clinicians evaluate whether the diagnostic process was adequate (Morrison, 2007). At a wider level, researchers and policy makers are interested in the effectiveness of diagnoses and continually investigate the causes and progress of mental disorders. Both are issues to which we will return in Sections 4.2.4 and 4.2.5, respectively, which discuss how clinical practice and research are part of a cycle that often takes several years to complete.

Assessment, on the other hand, refers to the series of steps and methods used to gather and evaluate relevant information about a patient, so that a diagnosis may be formulated and an appropriate treatment may be recommended. During the assessment, the clinician will learn about the person and obtain detailed information about their past and present circumstances in a systematic way.

As you will see in greater detail in Section 4.3.2, the assessment will typically include a clinical interview and, whenever necessary, further medical and psychological tests to help the clinician address a referral request that is usually generated by a general practitioner, or GP. In the UK, GPs are the equivalent of family doctors in other countries. **Referral** is a case that has been sent to a mental health specialist (see Box 4.1) for further investigation, who is usually asked to answer a question: for example, 'Is the patient clinically depressed?' Further tests may also help the clinician discriminate between 'competing' diagnoses as the assessment progresses. We will return to this issue later in Section 4.3.4, dedicated to differential diagnosis. The aim of the assessment and diagnosis process is to produce a case formulation that presents a theory, or a conceptualisation, of the patient's current state. We will also return to this phase of the process later, in Section 4.3.6.

■   What is the relationship between diagnosis and assessment?

☐   Diagnosis is the process used to find out whether a person's signs and symptoms fit a particular syndrome in a clinically significant way; that is, it is causing them significant distress, disability and/or risk. The assessment is part of the diagnostic process.

■   What is the difference between a sign, a symptom and a syndrome?

☐   A sign is an objective indication of mental disease that may be noticed by others. A symptom is an uncomfortable sensation reported by the person that indicates a change in the way they function: for example, 'I can't sleep at night'. A syndrome refers to a group of symptoms and signs occurring in a specific pattern that suggests the existence of a disorder.

Mental health teams

In the UK, mental health patients are assessed and diagnosed by mental health teams that usually include psychiatrists, clinical psychologists, mental health nurses, social workers and occupational therapists (see Box 4.1 and Figure 4.1). Patients may generally be assessed either by a psychiatrist, a clinical psychologist or a mental health nurse but in the remainder of the chapter, the term 'clinician' (or clinical psychologist) will be used to refer to all of these roles.

Box 4.1 Who is who in a mental health team?

A **psychiatrist** is a medical doctor with special training in mental illnesses and emotional problems. If patients need to take medication, a psychiatrist will be responsible for arranging this.

A **clinical psychologist** has a degree in psychology and a further three years' training in clinical psychology. They assess patients and give psychological treatments. They will usually meet with patients for a number of sessions to talk through their feelings, thinking and behaving.

Many psychiatrists and most clinical psychologists have also been trained in psychotherapy. **Psychotherapy** is the treatment of mental and emotional disorders through the use of psychological techniques designed to encourage communication of conflicts and gain insight into problems. The goal of psychotherapy is to bring relief of symptoms and changes in behaviour leading to improved social and vocational functioning, and personality growth.

Mental health nurses undergo a 3–4-year training programme specific to caring for patients with mental health issues. They can help patients talk through problems and give practical advice and support. They can also give medicines and keep an eye on their effects.

Social workers help people to talk through their problems, give them practical advice and emotional support and provide some psychological treatments. They work in the community and are able to give expert practical help with money, housing problems and other entitlements.

Occupational therapists help people to get back to doing the practical things of everyday life. They may help patients work out what they can and cannot do, and provide advice and support on their road to becoming independent.

Figure 4.1 A multidisciplinary team consists of psychiatrists, mental health nurses, clinical psychologists, social workers and occupational therapists, who provide assessment, care and treatment.

Activity 4.1 The impact of a diagnosis in mental health

(L.O 4.3) Allow 15 minutes

Make some notes about how a person might feel about receiving a diagnosis of a mental illness and the possible advantages and disadvantages of receiving such a diagnosis.

The theories behind mental health diagnoses have changed considerably in the last millennia and will probably continue to change in the foreseeable future, reflecting greater understanding of mental disorders as well as changes in the social norms; that is, what societies accept as 'normal'. But what has been the logic behind the diagnosis of mental illness so far? We turn to this question in the next section, beginning with a brief history of the origins of diagnoses.

4.2 The logic of diagnosis

4.2.1 The Greeks and *melas kholé*

The recognition and classification of mental disorders have a long and interesting history reaching back into antiquity. Humoral theory (or humoralism), a concept first introduced in Greek medicine by Hippocrates around 400 BC (see also Section 1.2.2), proposed that the internal cavities of the human body were filled with four basic substances, or humours, identified as black bile, yellow bile, phlegm and blood. The term 'humour' derives from the Greek word *chymos*, literally meaning juice, sap or, metaphorically, flavour. The Greeks believed that mental disorders were caused by the imbalance of these humours, or *dyskrasia*, which literally means 'bad mixture'. Examples of mental disorders described then included melancholy (sadness), hysteria (a state of violent mental agitation) and phobia (irrational, intense fear).

Hippocrates and later Galen (AD 131–200), believed that the humours affected a range of human moods, emotions and behaviours in such a way that each of the four humours was thought to correspond to a different type of personality or temperament (Figure 4.2): melancholic (the thoughtful ponderers), sanguine (the light-hearted and confident), choleric (the doers) and phlegmatic (the kind and shy).

Each of the temperaments was thought to have positive and negative qualities, which became more or less 'powered' by humoral imbalances. The interpretation of humoral imbalances was key to the diagnosis of mental diseases and the choice of a treatment. The diagnostic term 'melancholy', for example, derives from the Greek words *melas* and *kholé*, literally meaning 'black bile', illustrating the type of humour thought to be excessive in this disorder.

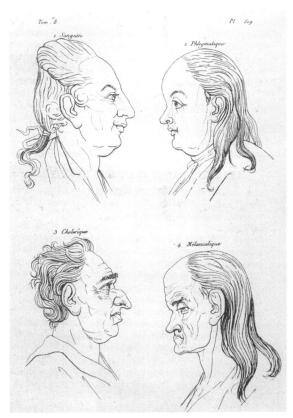

Figure 4.2 The four temperaments used to aid diagnosis (top row: sanguine and phlegmatic; bottom row: choleric and melancholic).

The term 'Ayurveda' derives from the Sanskrit (a historic Indo-Aryan language) *ayus*, 'life' and *veda*, 'science'.

It should be noted that Western diagnostic systems have coexisted with other ancient systems such as Ayurveda and Chinese acupuncture. Ayurveda is a system of traditional medicine that originated in India and is practised in other parts of the world as a form of alternative medicine. It emphasises the prevention of disease, rejuvenation of bodily systems and the extension of the lifespan. Acupuncture, on the other hand, is an ancient Chinese technique that regulates the flow of 'life energy' (or *qi*, pronounced ki) in the body by inserting and manipulating thin needles into various points to relieve pain or for other therapeutic purposes.

In the West, 'humoral' medicine remained popular for two millennia. It was adopted by Roman and Muslim physicians and respected by European doctors until the 18th century, when it was abandoned in favour of more modern approaches to mental disorders, as discussed in the next section.

4.2.2 The classification of mental disorders from the 18th century to the present

A paradigm is a theoretical framework of any kind used to make sense of reality.

In contrast to the humoral model of holistic 'flows' and fluid 'imbalances' in the body, mid-18th century physicians became interested in the dissection and scrutiny of specific organs and tissues. This **paradigm** shift was helped by a new instrument (the microscope) that extended the researchers' sight and paved the way for germ theory and the identification (and classification) of the underlying causes of some illnesses. From this new perspective, disease was seen as a disruption caused by the entry of microbes into the body. Accordingly, the study of illnesses began to concentrate on the biological and biochemical enquiry of the workings of body parts and the detection of specific and invisible germs that could explain their causes.

From then onwards, mental health care in Western countries adopted what is known as the biomedical model (see also Section 1.2.3), which concentrated on conquering and curing disease. The consequence of this shift was a newly acquired focus on disease, rather than the whole person, and the mission to discriminate between what is 'normal' and 'pathological' whilst making judgements about the boundary between them.

Within this context, modern approaches to the classification of mental disorders derive largely from the pioneering work of the German psychiatrist Emil Kraepelin (Figure 4.3). In line with the dominant 'biological' approach of his time, Kraepelin (in 1899) suggested that both physical and mental disorders should be classified in similar ways, or using the same taxonomy. **Taxonomy** – from the Greek, *taxis* (arrangement) and *nomia* (method) – means method of arrangement. The new method enabled him to re-classify psychosis into two subgroups, effectively discriminating, for the first time, between dementia praecox (now known as schizophrenia) and **manic-depressive psychosis** (an earlier term for bipolar disorder that is no longer used). These three diagnostic categories are described next.

Figure 4.3 Emil Kraepelin (1856–1926), the founder of contemporary scientific psychiatry.

The term psychosis was coined by Ernst von Feuchtersleben in 1845 and used to distinguish disorders then believed to be those of the mind, as opposed to neurosis, which were thought to be those of the brain (as described in Chapters 1 to 3, this dualistic distinction has now been abandoned). Currently,

psychosis describes a mental condition involving a 'loss of contact with reality', where somebody is unable to distinguish between reality and their imagination: for example, thinking that you are Napoleon, the new Messiah, or a reincarnation of John Lennon. People with psychosis often experience hallucinations (hearing or seeing things that do not exist) and delusions (believing in things that have not happened or are untrue). Could this be what the famous Norwegian painter Edvard Munch (1863–1944) was trying to depict in *The Scream* (Figure 4.4)? Psychosis can be caused by psychological conditions, medical conditions, or abuse of substances such as alcohol or drugs.

Figure 4.4 Edvard Munch's *The Scream* (1893). Could it be interpreted as depicting loss of contact with reality?

Schizophrenia comes from the Greek *skhizein* (to split) and *phren* (mind) and is a particular type of psychosis. It is a long-lasting, or chronic, mental health disorder. People with schizophrenia experience a range of different psychological symptoms, including hallucinations, delusions and disorganised thinking. They may, for example, hear voices other people don't hear. Also, they may believe other people are reading their minds, controlling their thoughts, or plotting to harm them. This can terrify people with the illness and make them withdrawn or extremely agitated. Onset of the symptoms typically occurs in young adulthood. You may recall the case of Angie, the 19-year-old who is frightened by voices she hears. Schizophrenia can be treated, and many people with this illness can lead full and productive lives (see Box 4.2a). There are no laboratory tests for schizophrenia and its exact cause is unknown. However, experts agree that schizophrenia may develop as a result of interplay between biological predisposition (for example, inheriting certain genes) and the kind of environment to which a person is exposed.

Bipolar disorder, also known as manic-depressive illness, is a disorder that causes unusual shifts in mood, energy, activity levels, and the ability to carry out day-to-day tasks. Symptoms of bipolar disorder include abnormally elevated and abnormally depressed states for a period of time in a way that interferes with functioning. For example, a person with bipolar disorder may believe that he or she has special powers or is a special person. Bipolar disorder symptoms can result in damaged relationships, poor job or school performance, and even suicide (see Box 4.2b). However, bipolar disorder can be treated, and people with this illness can lead full and productive lives. We will return to this theme in Section 4.3 and again in Chapter 2 of Book 2.

Figure 4.5 John Forbes Nash Jr (1928–), American mathematician and Nobel Prize winner.

Box 4.2 Famous people with mental disorders

(a) From schizophrenia to the Nobel Prize: the case of John Nash Jr

John Nash Jr (Figure 4.5) is an American mathematician who has faced a lifelong battle with schizophrenia. Despite having stopped taking his prescribed medication, Nash continued his studies and was awarded the Nobel Prize in Economic Sciences in 1994 with two others. He was known at Princeton University, New Jersey, where his reclusive, ghost-like figure could be seen roaming around, writing complex mathematical equations on the boards of empty classrooms. His struggle was well-documented in the book *A Beautiful Mind*, by Sylvia Nasar, which was later adapted into a film of the same name.

(b) Virginia Woolf and bipolar disorder

Virginia Woolf (Figure 4.6), the British novelist known for her creative insight into human nature, experienced the mood swings typical of bipolar disorder most of her life. She received comfort, care and understanding from friends and family, and never had to face institutionalisation, the only medical treatment available in those days. Her cause of death was determined as 'suicide, whilst the balance of her mind was disturbed'. She drowned herself in the river Ouse, near her home in Rodmell, East Sussex. The onset of World War II, the destruction of her London home during the Blitz, and the cool reception given to her most recent work are thought to have worsened her condition.

Figure 4.6 Virginia Woolf, British novelist (1882–1941).

Kraepelin's new classification system represented a significant breakthrough that enabled clinicians to predict the course and outcome of some mental disorders. For example, he proposed that dementia praecox was primarily a disorder of intellectual functioning, believed to be caused by a chemical imbalance in the brain, and manic-depressive psychosis (as it was known then) was a disorder of the person's mood, caused by an irregularity in the body's metabolism.

Consequently, clinicians could predict different courses for dementia praecox and mania. They believed, for example, that dementia praecox would lead to irreversible mental decline, without possible recovery, whereas people suffering from manic depression would experience the illness intermittently (with acute episodes of extreme activity, or mania, followed by relatively symptom-free intervals), with no lasting deterioration of intellectual functioning.

The Swiss psychiatrist Eugen Bleuler (1857–1939) later renamed dementia praecox as schizophrenia.

■ What was Kraepelin's scientific legacy?

☐ Kraepelin's new classification system enabled clinicians to predict the course and outcome of some mental disorders.

Some of Kraepelin's predictions were, however, inaccurate. For example, dementia praecox does not necessarily lead to irreversible mental decline as he had predicted. Yet, modern classification systems such as the *Diagnostic and Statistical Manual of Mental Disorders* and the *International Statistical Classification of Diseases and Related Health Problems* are still largely based on his initial discrimination between psychotic symptoms. The next section introduces you to the logic behind these modern classification systems for mental disorders.

Figure 4.7 The DSM-IV-TR, the fourth edition with text revised (TR), published in 2000.

4.2.3 Tools for diagnosis in the 20th century: the age of the DSM and the ICD

Modern classification systems for mental disorders have developed into tightly constrained diagnostic categories in an attempt to make the process of diagnosis as thorough, systematic and objective as possible. In 1952, the American Psychiatric Association published their first list of the major diagnostic categories for mental disorders, known as the *Diagnostic and Statistical Manual of Mental Disorders*, or DSM-I, which is currently in its fourth edition, the DSM-IV-TR (Figure 4.7), published in 2000 (APA, 2000). The fifth edition of the DSM, the DSM-V, is expected in 2013. The DSM revisions have been based on field trials (i.e. were tested by specialists in clinical contexts), analysis of data sets and systematic reviews of the research literature, whilst seeking greater objectivity, diagnostic precision and reliability, an issue to which we will return in Section 4.2.4.

The *International Statistical Classification of Diseases and Related Health Problems*, or ICD, published by the World Health Organization (WHO), also includes a section classifying mental and behavioural disorders. Like the DSM, the ICD is revised periodically, using similar methodologies, and is currently in its tenth revision (or ICD-10; Figure 4.8), first published in 1994 (WHO, 1994). The ICD-6, published in 1949, was the first of the ICD series to contain a section on mental disorders. The eleventh revision of the ICD, or ICD-11, is planned for 2015.

Since the 1990s, the American Psychiatric Association and the World Health Organization have worked together to bring the DSM and the relevant sections of ICD into concordance, and both manuals seek to use the same codes, although some differences remain. Both diagnostic systems are used, in varying degrees, in several countries around the world.

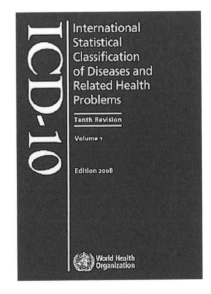

Figure 4.8 The ICD-10, the tenth revision, published by the World Health Organization in 1994.

However, a recent international survey of 205 psychiatrists in 66 countries, across all continents, comparing use of the ICD and the DSM has found that the ICD-10 was more frequently used and more valued for clinical diagnosis and training whereas the DSM-IV-TR was more valued for research (Mezzich, 2002). Yet, the DSM remains the most used diagnostic system in the USA and in the UK, and therefore we will be giving it more attention in this chapter.

Currently, the DSM-IV-TR includes 297 diagnostic categories of mental disorders and the increasing trend continues, as new categories such as **binge eating disorder** and **passive-aggressive personality disorder** are currently being considered for introduction in the DSM-V (expected in 2013). Binge eating disorder is characterised by compulsive overeating in which people consume vast amounts of food whilst feeling out of control and powerless to stop. Passive-aggressive personality disorder is a passive, sometimes systematic resistance to following through with expectations in interpersonal or occupational situations by means of passive activities such as lateness, procrastination, forgetfulness and intentional inefficiency.

You may think that 297 diagnostic categories is a remarkably high number. However, the ICD-10 currently lists 458 different types of mental disorders, which highlights differences in how diagnoses are obtained. In the last 20 years alone, between the publication of the DSM-III in 1980 and the DSM-IV-TR in 2000, 32 new diagnostic categories were created (see Table 4.1).

Table 4.1 Number of diagnostic categories of mental disorders per DSM edition. Source: Pincus et al. (1992).

DSM edition (year of publication)	Number of categories
DSM I (1952)	106
DSM-II (1968)	182
DSM-III (1980)	265
DSM-III-R (Revised; 1987)	292
DSM-IV-TR (Text Revised; 2000)	297

The diagnostic category corresponding to **autism** (or autistic spectrum disorder), for example, was only introduced in the DSM-III in 1980. Autistic spectrum disorder is characterised by impaired social interaction and communication abilities, as well as restricted activities and interests.

At the same time, evidence that some diagnostic categories have been discarded for lack of evidence to support them suggests the possibility that new 'disorders' are being artificially created. For example, the DSM-III (1980) listed two types of substance-use disorders (substance abuse and substance dependence) but the former was later excluded because clinicians had difficulties in differentiating between them effectively (Rounsaville et al., 1987). Another example of arguably unjustified 'category proliferation' is the distinction between attention-deficit disorder (a condition that is characterised by poor attention and distractibility and/or hyperactive and impulsive behaviours) 'with' and 'without hyperactivity', which was later dropped for lack of evidence to support the difference. Maj (2005) has highlighted the potential consequences of the current proliferation of diagnostic categories:

> If demarcations are made where they do not exist in nature, the probability that several diagnoses have to be made in an individual case will obviously increase.

(Maj, 2005; p. 182)

We will return to this issue and its impact in Section 4.3.5, dedicated to the identification of possible comorbid diagnoses, which refer to the presence of more than one diagnosis in the same person.

You should also note that society's view about specific habits has changed considerably in the last decades, which has also had an impact in the classification of diagnostic categories. For example, whereas years ago smoking and addiction to tobacco was not viewed as a disorder, it is currently listed under the category of 'substance-related disorders'.

■   The number of diagnostic categories in the DSM has increased over the years (Table 4.1). What can you conclude from this trend?

☐   Knowledge about diagnosis is constantly evolving. Evolution in the diagnosis of mental disorders generally reflects greater understanding of disorders as well as the influence of social norms. However, it is also possible that new 'disorders' are being artificially created.

Beyond the introduction of clearer diagnostic categories, the DSM-III (1980) and subsequent editions have also marked a clear shift from the previous biomedical, rather Kraepelian, approach to mental health discussed in Section 4.2.2, to include a multi-axial system that allows the evaluation of the person's current biological, psychological and social conditions on five different dimensions (or axes). The next section discusses how the five axes currently invite and enable the clinician to evaluate the person being diagnosed as a whole.

The DSM's five axes

The DSM specifies five dimensions along which a clinician assesses the person's behaviour. The five axes integrate different aspects of disorder or disability, inviting clinicians and researchers to take a broad view asserting that mental illness cannot be explained by simply looking at 'biological' factors alone, as had been proposed by Kraepelin. Hence, the five axes are designed to classify not only the person's mental disorder (Axes I and II) but also to evaluate their physical health (Axis III), the psychosocial and environmental problems in the person's life (Axis IV), and the degree of impairment in the person's mental health and ability to interact with society and care for themself (Axis V). Although, in practice, most clinicians tend to focus exclusively on Axes I and II, it is still worth introducing you to the five axes so that you may appreciate their scope and relevance.

Axis I refers broadly to the main disorder requiring immediate attention: for example, a major depressive episode, an exacerbation of schizophrenia, or a flare-up of panic disorder. Patients seek clinical help because of an Axis I disorder. The clinician will also note whether the disorder is acute or chronic. Whereas acute disorders are recent and have an abrupt onset of severe symptoms, chronic disorders last for long periods of time. Axis I disorders include depression, anxiety disorders, phobias, schizophrenia and bipolar disorder.

The term 'mental retardation' has been used in the USA, and some other parts of the world, with essentially the same meaning as intellectual disability. The term is no longer in use in the USA or the UK.

Axis II should specify whether there might be an underlying personality condition causing the abnormal behaviour. The clinician would list mental retardation (a DSM term) or any personality disorders, such as borderline personality disorder, or BPD, a serious mental illness characterised by pervasive instability in moods, interpersonal relationships, self-image and behaviour. These are listed in Axis II because they are life-long conditions, whereas most of the conditions listed in Axis I tend to come and go during the person's lifetime. Axes I and II are therefore differentiated so that clinicians may be able to detect whether an Axis II disorder is also involved. This generally indicates that the treatment may be more difficult.

On Axis III, the clinician would note any acute medical condition that may be affecting the person. For example, although there are no biological tests that confirm bipolar disorder, a patient with suspected bipolar disorder would typically be subjected to tests to exclude medical illnesses such as hypo- or hyperthyroidism (under- or overactivity of the thyroid gland), which could partially explain the behaviour. Crucially, the clinician should know whether the person is taking any other drugs or substances that may affect prescribed treatment drugs.

On Axis IV, the clinician would note any social situations or environmental factors that are causing the abnormal behaviour and rate their severity, as these may affect the type of treatment that is indicated. It is important to note that these stressors can act as causes of (or be caused by) mental disorders. An example of a powerful stressor is bereavement, as you will see later in Section 4.3.1 (Vignette 4.1). On Axis V, the clinician would rate the levels at which the person is able to function in his or her daily life, considering social relationships, **adaptive functioning** and even leisure time, using the Global Assessment of Functioning (GAF) scale. Some examples of this scale are shown in Box 4.3. Adaptive functioning is the ability to interact with society on all levels whilst caring effectively for one's self, showing willingness to practise skills and pursue opportunities for improvement on all levels.

Box 4.3 The global assessment of functioning (GAF) scale – some examples

The GAF is a numeric scale (0–100) used by mental health clinicians and physicians to rate subjectively the social, occupational and psychological functioning of adults: for instance, how well or adaptively one is meeting various problems in living. Here are reproduced some examples only.

81–90: Absent or minimal symptoms; good functioning in all areas.

71–80: If symptoms are present they are transient and expectable reactions to psychosocial stresses; only slight impairment in social, occupational or school functioning.

[…]

31–40: Some impairment in reality testing or communication OR major impairment in several areas.

21–30: Behaviour is influenced by delusions or hallucinations OR serious impairment in communications or judgement OR inability to function in all areas.

11–20: Some danger of hurting self or others OR occasionally fails to maintain minimal personal hygiene OR gross impairment in communication.

1–10: Persistent danger of severely hurting self or others OR inability to maintain minimum personal hygiene OR serious suicidal act with clear expectation of death.

■ Is antisocial personality disorder listed in Axis I or II? Why?

☐ It is listed in Axis II because it is a life-long condition, not a transient one.

The modern diagnostic classification systems have attracted praise as well as controversy and criticism, in equal measure. This is a crucial issue to which we will return later in Section 4.2.6, dedicated to the potential dangers of diagnosing mental illness, and also in the first chapter of Book 2 where the same drawbacks are discussed in the context of depression and anxiety. Meanwhile, however, with an increasing number of mental illnesses listed, an obvious question to ask is whether the DSM has improved the accuracy of diagnosis. We turn to this question in the next section.

4.2.4 Has the DSM improved how diagnoses are made?

The question of whether transformations in the DSM have improved how diagnoses are made relates directly to issues of validity and reliability. These are terms you need to understand before we can move on. As you will see throughout this chapter, these two terms will remain central to assessment and diagnosis because they enable clinicians to make more reliable diagnostic judgements, and researchers to be reasonably confident that they are measuring mental phenomena as objectively as possible.

Validity determines whether an evaluation procedure (often a test) truly measures what it is intended to measure. In other words, is the measurement accurate and are the results useful and truthful or are the authors measuring something else? Valid findings are those that, through systematic or scientific research, have been proven to be sound or well established. This remains, however, a complex concept because it often involves the interpretation of subjective traits that cannot be observed, or measured, overtly. We will return to this issue and its implications for diagnosing mental disorders in Section 4.2.6.

Consider, for example, the validity of multiple-choice exams given to students. These exams are designed to measure the students' knowledge and understanding of relevant course contents. However, it is also possible that, in some cases, they may instead measure some students' specific expertise in handling multiple-choice examination situations and their ability to second-guess the examiner or recognise any distracters in the questions. So a multiple-choice examination with validity would have to measure knowledge of course contents and not the ability to second-guess the examiner.

At a deeper level, validity indicates the strength of the results obtained. Can the authors confidently say that they are really 'identifying' or 'measuring', say, proneness to depression using a questionnaire? If this questionnaire has validity, people who obtain different scores in this test can be said to differ in depression proneness. However, the same test would lose its validity if clinicians decided to use it to assess people who are clinically depressed.

Reliability, on the other hand, is the extent to which an evaluation or measuring procedure yields the same results, or leads to the same conclusions, when used by different clinicians. This is also known as inter-rater, or inter-judge, reliability. Reliability is about precision and consistency. For example, if you want to measure the area of a room, a measuring tape will be more reliable than an elastic band, the length of which depends on how taut the band is held.

The question of whether the DSM has increased the reliability of diagnostic judgements can be illustrated using the description of manic depression (or bipolar disorder) as an example. If you compare the definitions of manic depression in the DSM-II (1968; see Box 4.4a) and in the DSM-IV-TR (2000; Box 4.4b) you will see that the description of manic episodes has become clearer and more precise, thus reducing uncertainty in diagnosing this condition. By comparison, the 'old' diagnostic criteria are too vague and, for this reason, probably too dependent on the clinician's interpretation of what may be regarded as a clinically significant episode.

Box 4.4 Comparing descriptions for the same diagnostic category

(a) Diagnostic criteria for a manic episode in the DSM-II (1968, p. 36)

Manic-depressive illness, manic type. This disorder consists exclusively of manic episodes. These episodes are characterised by excessive elation, irritability, talkativeness, flight of ideas, and accelerated speech and motor activity. (Brief periods of depression sometimes occur, but they are never true depressive episodes.)

(b) Diagnostic criteria for a manic episode in the DSM-IV-TR (2000, p. 236)

A – A distinct period of abnormality and persistently elevated, expansive, or irritable mood, lasting at least one week (or any duration if hospitalisation is necessary).

B – During the period of mood disturbance, three (or more) of the following symptoms have persisted (four if the mood is only irritable) and have been present to a significant degree:

1 inflated self-esteem or grandiosity

2 decreased need for sleep (e.g. feels rested after only three hours of sleep)

3 more talkative than usual or pressure to keep talking

4 flight of ideas or subjective experience that thoughts are racing

5 distractibility (i.e. attention too easily drawn to unimportant or irrelevant external stimuli)

6 increase in goal-directed activity (either socially, at work or school, or sexually) or psychomotor agitation

7 excessive involvement in pleasurable activities that have a high potential for painful consequences (e.g. engaging in unrestrained buying sprees, sexual indiscretions or foolish business investments).

C – The symptoms do not meet criteria for a mixed episode (i.e. a condition during which symptoms of mania and depression occur simultaneously).

D – The mood disturbance is sufficiently severe to cause marked impairment in occupational functioning, or in unusual social activities or relationships with others, or to necessitate hospitalisation to prevent harm to self or others, or there are psychotic features (see Section 4.2.2).

E – The symptoms are not due to the direct physiological effects of a substance (e.g. a drug abuse, a medication or other treatment) or a general medical condition (e.g. hyperthyroidism).

It should be noted, however, that some diagnostic categories can be more reliable than others and this depends on the disorder being diagnosed. For instance, patients with OCD (Axis I) may display behaviours that are fairly constant and relatively easy to identify such as the compulsion to wash their hands several times a day. On the other hand, patients with borderline personality disorder (BPD, Axis II) may display behaviours that are more complex, variable and less overt, which makes this disorder more difficult to identify.

Figure 4.9 illustrates the relationship between measurements that can be reliable but not valid (on the left), neither valid nor reliable (centre), or valid and reliable (right). Some measurements may be reliable but not valid, which means that they consistently measure a trait that is not what the researchers intended to measure. In other words, they miss the target (left). However, tests cannot be valid if they are not reliable (centre). Finally, tests that are both valid and reliable tend to hit the target by measuring what they were intended to measure in a consistent way (right).

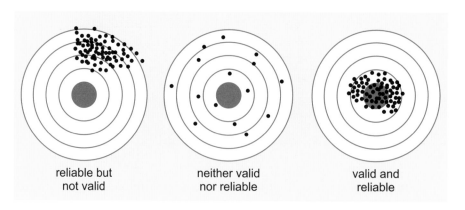

Figure 4.9 Illustrating the relationship between validity and reliability.

■ How has the DSM-IV-TR (published in 2000) improved the reliability of diagnostic judgements in comparison with the DSM-II (published in 1968)?

☐ The new diagnostic criteria for manic episodes are, by comparison, clearly spelt out and have the additional advantage of including illustrative examples, which were absent in the DSM-II.

The diagnostic categories listed in the DSM are not only important in the consulting room. They are also used by external agencies that interact with mental health institutions, such as health insurance companies, psychiatric drug regulation agencies, pharmaceutical companies, policy makers and courts of law. Crucially, the DSM's diagnostic categories form the basis for systematic research studies, as discussed in the next section.

4.2.5 Researching mental health

Using the same diagnostic definitions enables researchers in different institutions all over the world to:

• collect data on numbers of cases in different categories of human populations (such as by age, sex and location), and

• compare the number of cases of specific mental illnesses or

• compare the effectiveness of mental health treatments, therapies or other interventions.

The experts refer to these different segments of the population as demographic categories and use them to study the occurrence, distribution and potential causes of mental illnesses in different groups of people around the world. This field of study, known as **epidemiology** (historically, the study of epidemics), is the essential basic science of public health, including mental health. It provides the logical framework for the facts that enable researchers to identify crucial mental health problems and to outline their dimensions.

Epidemiological methods are used to define these problems; to classify, identify and elucidate their causes; and to plan and evaluate rational control measures. These methods enable researchers to ask questions such as: do women get more depressed than men? Or, why is schizophrenia diagnosed more often in one region of the globe in comparison to another?

The basis of epidemiological research is the comparison of groups of people mainly through the use of correlational studies (see Box 4.5). Figure 4.10, for example, compares the incidence and prevalence rates (defined below) for schizophrenia in men and women (demographic category: sex) by latitude (demographic category: location), including data from 68 studies in 27 countries distributed in three different latitude bands (Saha et al., 2006):

- low band (Equator to 30°; Barbados, Brazil, India, Pakistan, Singapore, Trinidad and Tobago)

- medium band (30° to 60°; Canada, China, Croatia, Denmark, France, Germany, Ireland, Italy, Jamaica, Japan, New Zealand, Spain, Sweden, the Netherlands, UK, USA)

- high band (above 60°; Canada, Finland, Greenland, Iceland, Norway, Russia, Sweden).

Different latitudes imply different climates, cultural habits and diets. Will such differences influence the prevalence and incidence of schizophrenia? 'Prevalence' and 'incidence' are terms commonly used by epidemiologists that you must understand before you can interpret Figures 4.10 and 4.11 (see also Box 4.5a). So, what do they mean?

Prevalence

Prevalence indicates the total number of people who have the condition (or disease) at a particular *point* in time, regardless of how long they have been affected. However, researchers usually prefer to work with **prevalence rates** as an indication of the total number of people who have the condition at a particular point in time, expressed as a *rate* per 1000 (or per 10 000, or per 100 000 or per million) of the population. Prevalence rates are thought to be more informative because they put the number of cases in the context of specific countries, enabling comparisons amongst different countries.

If you read, for example, that there are 35 000 and 260 000 people with schizophrenia in Croatia and Canada, respectively (these are known as raw numbers), you might be temped to conclude that there is a higher proportion of people in Canada with schizophrenia than in Croatia. However, direct comparisons must take into account the populations in each country and this is precisely what prevalence rates do. So, in this case, the prevalence rates provided by the World Health Organization (WHO) indicate that these two countries have similar prevalence rates for schizophrenia.

■   Why are prevalence rates generally more useful than prevalence?

☐   Because prevalence rates enable the comparison of epidemiological data across different countries with different population sizes.

Incidence

Incidence, on the other hand indicates the number of *new* cases diagnosed in a population in a given period, usually one year. The key word is new. Again, to facilitate comparisons across different countries with varying population sizes, epidemiologists prefer to focus on **incidence rates** which are the number of new cases in a given period, usually a year, expressed as a rate per 1000 (or per 10 000, or per 100 000 or per million) of the population. Increasing incidence rates reveal an increasing trend, which, in due course, will increase the prevalence rates. Figure 4.10 shows a significantly higher prevalence rate for schizophrenia for both sexes in high latitude countries such as Sweden, in comparison with low latitude countries like Brazil.

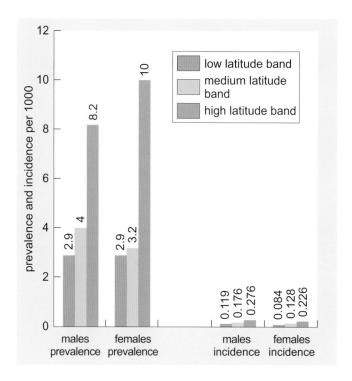

Figure 4.10 Prevalence (per 1000) and incidence (per 1000) of schizophrenia by latitude band.

■ How can you interpret the incidence rate results also presented in Figure 4.10?

☐ The number of new cases of schizophrenia being diagnosed in the high latitude band countries is nearly double that in medium latitude band countries and nearly three times that in counties at low latitude.

Figure 4.11 shows data from a study in the USA comparing trends in the outpatient diagnosis and treatment of bipolar disorder in young people (aged 0 to 19 years) and adults (aged 20 or above; Moreno et al., 2007). The authors estimated the bipolar disorder visit rates per 100 000 population as a proportion of total clinic-based visits (which includes all other disorders) from 1994 to 2003. The results show that, during the same period, the increase in percentage of visits with a diagnosis of bipolar disorder increased significantly faster in the young people group, in comparison with the adults.

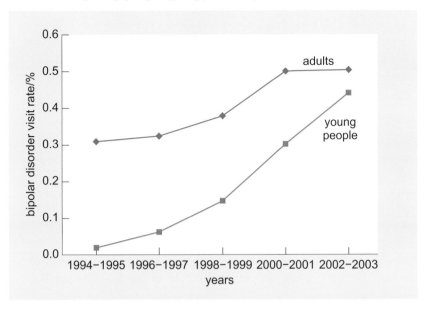

Figure 4.11 US trends in visits with a diagnosis of bipolar disorder as a percentage of total clinic-based visits by young people (aged 0–19 years) and adults (aged 20 years or above).

■ How can you critically interpret the results presented in Figure 4.11?

☐ Within about 10 years, the figures show an alarming increase in clinic-based visits with a diagnosis of childhood and adolescent bipolar disorder. This might be the manifestation of a genuine increase due, for example, to environmental factors. However, this could also indicate that either bipolar disorder was historically under-diagnosed in this age group, a problem that has now been rectified, or bipolar disorder is now being over-diagnosed in this age group. We will return to this issue in Section 4.2.6, dedicated to the potential dangers of diagnosis.

Box 4.5 Research Methods: Describing data and correlational studies

(a) Describing data

Graphs and charts are used to illustrate information, so it is important to be able to interpret them correctly. Often, the authors of an article will attempt to emphasise the point they are trying to make by presenting the facts and figures in such a way as to confirm their argument. This is a commonly used approach, which means that it is essential to examine graphs and charts used very carefully. When you are asked to describe data, it is important to use all the information given in the graph. You should start by looking at the axis labels on the graph and the title (if there is one). For example, the graph in Figure 4.11 shows time along the horizontal axis in years and the bipolar disorder visit rates expressed as a proportion of total visit rates to outpatient clinics along the vertical axis. To describe the data, you need to describe the shape of the lines and the relationship between the lines that you see. For example, in Figure 4.11 the 'adults' line shows an increase in visit rates for bipolar disorder from 1994 to 2000 where it levels out with no further increase between 2000 and 2003. By contrast, the 'young people' line shows a small increase between 1994 and 1998 and then a very much larger increase between 1999 and 2003.

(b) Correlational studies

Epidemiologists look for *relationships* between different groups of people and the occurrence of illness. The studies can be *cross-sectional*, in which different groups of people are compared at one moment in time. An example of this is the prevalence and incidence rates of schizophrenia in different populations according to their latitude band, shown in Figure 4.10. Alternatively, researchers can analyse trends *longitudinally*, in which a population is studied at different times. For example, Figure 4.11 shows the percentage of outpatient visits with a diagnosis of bipolar disorder in the US population, from 1994 to 2003. Other smaller scale longitudinal studies might follow the same group of individuals over a period of time: for example, to monitor the emergence of a mental health disorder in a group of individuals thought to be at risk of developing the disorder.

The types of studies described above are **correlational studies**, where the researchers are looking for a correlation, or relationship, between two variables. Correlational studies provide a snapshot of how things are in the real world. They provide useful information about the occurrence of health problems in particular groups of people and may provide evidence for further hypotheses about the causes of particular illnesses. They differ from the **experimental method**, in which the experimenter manipulates variables and participants are allocated into groups. Therefore a potential drawback to correlational studies is that there may be many other variables, apart from those under investigation, which cannot be controlled by the researchers.

The strength of a relationship between two variables can be measured by plotting the results onto a graph and analysing how close the points are to a straight line. The numerical measure of this strength of relationship is known as the **correlation coefficient**, expressed as a number between 1.0 and −1.0 and denoted by the symbol r.

Look back at Figure 1.10. This shows the relationship between income inequality and the prevalence of mental illness. You can see that the points on the graph fall fairly well into a straight line, with one or two outliers. The researchers report that $r = 0.73$ for this study, which suggests a strong relationship between the variables. This is a positive correlation in that as one variable increases, so does the other variable. If one variable decreases whilst the other increases, this is known as a negative correlation, and is denoted by a minus sign (e.g. −0.73). The closer the value of r is to 1.0 or −1.0, the higher the strength of correlation.

However, care must be taken in the interpretation of correlations. A strong correlation does not necessarily mean that one variable has *caused* the other. A correlation highlights a relationship, but does not imply causality, or the direction of that causality. There may be another variable, for example, that has had an effect on both variables in the study.

Finally, it should be pointed out that correlational studies are not only used in the field of epidemiology. Many health researchers and psychologists use correlational studies in order to assess the relationship between one variable and another. As you work through SDK228, you will read about many such studies that have been performed in laboratory or natural settings. An example is the correlation between various types of pathology in Alzheimer's disease and the severity of the illness, which you will read about in Book 4.

So far, from Kraepelin to the recent revisions of the DSM (and the ICD), the development of diagnostic category systems has been based on the belief that:

- people with mental health problems present signs and symptoms
- these signs and symptoms can be categorised and that, implicitly
- this categorisation can be used to distinguish those with or without mental disorders.

But is this a valid and reliable principle that may be followed blindly? Or are there any drawbacks associated with discriminating the 'sane' from the 'insane'? Well, it seems there are (and many). So, in the next section, we will be addressing the other side of the argument.

4.2.6 The potential dangers of diagnosis

The difficulties of distinguishing the 'normal' from the 'abnormal' are constantly illustrated by high profile murder trials in countries such as the USA or the UK, where authoritative psychiatrists for the prosecution on the matter of the defendant's sanity contradict eminent psychiatrists for the defence. Also, what is viewed as 'normal' in one culture may be seen as quite 'aberrant' in another (Benedict, 1934; Canino and Alegria, 2008; Hwang et al., 2008).

Consider, for example, that a woman wearing a mini-skirt walks in downtown Paris with friends, and then imagine the same scene taking place in downtown Kabul, Afghanistan's capital. Yet, the DSM is being used around the world. Is it then possible that notions of 'normality' and 'abnormality' may not be quite as accurate or universal as some people believe them to be? If so, what could be the consequences of such variability for diagnosing mental illness?

Thomas Szasz (1994) has argued that the decision to label someone with a mental disorder is so inherently biased that the whole system of diagnosis should be abandoned. The risk, he suggested, is that diagnoses can be used to dispose of people who do not 'fit' in a society that does not accept their alternative ways of behaving and looking at the world (see Box 4.6a).

But even those who disagree with Szasz's view (taken as radical by many) would probably recognise the great dangers of labelling behaviours (or people) as 'abnormal'. Beyond being treated differently by society, which has significant personal and social implications, the differential treatment is likely to continue long after the person has stopped exhibiting the behaviours labelled as abnormal. Note, incidentally, that the word 'insane' has a limited application, and a clear distinction should be made between labelling someone as 'mentally ill' or 'insane'. For example, most people with depression, anxiety, OCD and bulimia are not considered 'insane' and so this term is best confined to acute states of extreme disorders. An example of such an acute state would be a hallucinatory period in a person with schizophrenia, featuring an evident loss of contact with reality.

Yet, although most people will probably recognise that the physically ill may heal, is society, and are mental health clinicians in particular, prepared to accept that mentally ill people can also recover? Unfortunately, the evidence suggests that the 'mentally ill' label continues to carry considerable stigma associated with it, as we will see next.

The role of the context

The psychologist David Rosenhan (1973) investigated the effects of diagnostic labelling in mental health contexts in a now classic study, showing that healthy pseudo-patients went undetected in mental hospitals for weeks (see Box 4.6b). So, if mental health professionals cannot distinguish between normal and abnormal behaviours, then the dangers of diagnostic labels are even greater in the hands of lay-people, concluded Rosenhan (1973). In other words, mental illness labels are so influential on the patient and relatives that diagnoses run the risk of acting as self-fulfilling prophecies. However, it should be noted that, at the time (i.e. in the 1970s), the relevant diagnostic categories were less reliable. You have also learnt that the DSM has improved its reliability since then (see Section 4.2.4).

Figure 4.12 Opal Petty in 1994.

Box 4.6 The burden of a psychiatric label

(a) The case of Opal Petty

Opal Petty (Figure 4.12) died in 2005, aged 86, after having spent 51 years of involuntary commitment in a state mental hospital in Texas. Opal Petty was probably of **borderline intelligence**, which meant she had the minimal intelligence quotient (IQ) required to be able to function normally and independently in the world; that is, without some form of institutional assistance. She began displaying strange behaviours as a teenager, including hallucinations and aggressiveness towards family members. She also wanted to go dancing, which was not approved of by her fundamentalist religious parents. When a church exorcism failed to correct the situation, she was diagnosed with schizophrenia and committed to a mental hospital. Her institutionalisation was to last until she was 67, when a distant relative requested her release. In 1989, four years after her 'rescue', she won a $505,000 verdict against the Texas Department of Mental Health and Mental Retardation for negligently subjecting her to 'institutionalisation syndrome'. The court noted that she had been variously diagnosed during her confinement as sometimes being schizophrenic or retarded and at other times as neither mentally ill nor retarded. Opal lived the last 20 years of her life with her family, apparently symptom-free.

(b) The Rosenhan experiment (1973): on being sane in insane places

David Rosenhan (Figure 4.13) and seven other 'pseudo-patients' were admitted to 12 different mental health hospitals in the USA claiming they had been hearing voices. During the interviews they told the truth about all other aspects of their lives, including the fact that they had never experienced mental disorders before. All (but one) were diagnosed with schizophrenia. However, upon admission, all pseudo-patients resumed their 'normal' behaviours and told the hospital staff that the voices had ceased. Crucially, even though the hospital reports uniformly indicated that the pseudo-patients were 'friendly' and 'exhibited no abnormal indications', none of the hospital staff detected their 'normality' – although several patients did. Also, although it took the pseudo-patients an average of 19 days (between 7 and 52 days) to leave, they could only be discharged with a diagnosis of schizophrenia 'in remission', which meant that the staff still believed they had schizophrenia.

Figure 4.13 David L. Rosenhan during the 1970s.

■ What can be concluded from Rosenhan's experiment?

☐ That it is not possible, or at least very difficult, to distinguish the 'sane' from the 'insane' in mental hospitals, where the meanings of behaviour can be easily misunderstood. So, context is crucial.

The role of expectations

Rosenhan's experiment infuriated the psychiatric profession so, in a follow-up experiment, he announced that he would be sending another group of pseudo-patients to one of the previous participating hospitals during the next three months. The staff in this particular hospital announced their doubts that such an error could take place in 'their' institution.

During the following months, the hospital staff reported that they were quite confident they had detected 41 such pseudo-patients, out of 193 admissions, and a further 43 were considered suspect. However, in an unexpected twist of events, Rosenhan revealed that this time, no pseudo-patients had been sent out at all (at least from his experiment). Meanwhile, however, the number of admissions had dropped considerably showing that expectations could influence the diagnostic process.

Figure 4.14 The psychologist Lauren Slater received varied diagnoses whilst replicating Rosenhan's (1973) experiment in 2003.

It should be noted that since Rosenhan's experiment more than 30 years ago, the mental health system in the USA (as well as in the UK) has changed considerably and today, the emphasis is on 'care in the community' through the work of mental health teams (see Box 4.1), which means that significantly fewer patients are admitted to mental hospitals. Secondly, it could be argued (as discussed in Section 4.2.4) that the DSM has, since then, enabled higher reliability in diagnostic judgements. However, recent evidence has again cast doubts on diagnosing mental illness. In 2003, the psychologist Lauren Slater (Figure 4.14) repeated Rosenhan's (1973) experiment and tried to check herself in as a pseudo-patient at various hospitals in California. Interestingly, although she was not admitted to hospital, she was nevertheless diagnosed with a range of conditions, including psychosis, depression and post-traumatic stress disorder (PTSD; Slater, 2004), thus becoming a recent (and high-profile) example of a false positive. (False positives and also false negatives are described in Box 4.7.)

Box 4.7 False positives and false negatives

A **false positive** is a result that is erroneously positive when a situation is normal. It is another way of saying that the diagnosis was, after all, inaccurate and the person does not actually have the disease. False positives should be avoided. First, the stigma associated with the 'label' may induce loss of self-esteem. Second, false positives lead to confusion and distraction from the real condition that may remain untreated. This means that 'false positive' patients may be receiving treatment that is unnecessary and delaying treatment that is needed. False positives are perhaps more likely to occur when clinicians use criteria that rest exclusively on signs and symptoms and overlook the context of the person. In the context of mental illness, **false negatives** are results of diagnoses where mental health problems are ignored or misdiagnosed as 'physical illness' and go untreated.

Source credibility

Additionally, there is evidence that clinicians may be particularly vulnerable to suggestions made by those regarded as 'experts' in the field (seen as credible sources of information), which further compromises the validity of diagnoses in mental health. This point was made by Temerlin (1970) in an experiment where a group of trained clinicians and non-clinicians (e.g. law students) listened to a taped interview of a man who seemed to be going through a particularly happy and vibrant period in his life. During the interview the man described his work as rewarding and promising, his relationships as satisfying and his marriage as happy and sexually gratifying. He was also free of symptoms that typically generate diagnoses of mental illness, such as depression, anxiety, psychosomatic symptoms, hostility, suspiciousness and thought disturbance.

After listening to the interview, the clinicians and non-clinicians were divided into two groups. The first group heard a respected 'authority' in the field say that the man seemed neurotic but was actually 'quite psychotic' (note that this was deliberately misleading information), and the second group heard the same authority say that the person was 'quite healthy'. The results revealed that the majority of the trained clinicians in the first group disregarded the information in the tape and agreed with the negative opinion stated by the 'authority' – and they were more influenced than the non-clinicians.

■ What do the results from Rosenhan's, Slater's and Temerlin's studies suggest in terms of the limitations of diagnoses in mental health?

□ Rosenhan's second experiment is instructive. It suggests that the tendency to diagnose 'sane' people as 'insane' can be reversed when professional prestige and diagnostic expertise are at stake. Beyond the context, Temerlin's (1970) experiment also shows that experts often influence clinicians' judgements, so expectations also seem to count. Thirty years later, despite the DSM improvements discussed in Section 4.2.4, Slater's (2004) evidence again raises concerns about the validity and reliability of mental health diagnoses.

This section began by mentioning the impact of cultural variability in diagnosing mental illness – an issue to which we now return. Could insensitivity to cultural context, and the relative meaning of the symptoms displayed, lead clinicians to misinterpret cultural differences in emotional expression and social behaviour as 'impaired'? We turn to this issue next.

Cultural issues

Loring and Powell (1988) showed that clinicians might be influenced by expectations about the patients' cultural background (i.e. race). They asked 290 psychiatrists to make a diagnosis based on a clear schizophrenic case description (Axis I) and a clear dependent personality disorder (Axis II). The race of the patient depicted was manipulated; that is, some psychiatrists were told that the patient was white, others were told the patient was black, and a third group simply didn't know.

The results revealed that correct diagnoses were most often given when no identifying information on the patient was included. Also, black patients were given more severe diagnoses, regardless of the race of the psychiatrist: 'Clinicians appear to ascribe violence, suspiciousness, and dangerousness to black clients even though the case studies are the same as the case studies for the white clients' (Loring and Powell, 1988). Finally, the authors found that paranoid schizophrenia was diagnosed more frequently in black patients by both black and white psychiatrists.

■ What essential issues about diagnosing are raised by the studies described above?

□ Taken together, the results of these studies suggest that clinicians can be vulnerable to suggestion and this may, in some cases, affect their judgement and interpretations. They can also be very resistant to changing entrenched expectations or preconceptions, particularly in contexts where they expect to encounter certain phenomena.

Activity 4.2 The practice of diagnosis: the clinician's perspective

(LOs 4.1–4.6) Allow 30 minutes

Now would be an ideal time to go to the multimedia map and listen to the audio of an interview with clinical psychologist: Neil Frude. Then follow the instructions in the activity.

This section discussed the logic of diagnosis, balancing the increased precision of the DSM (which has enabled clinical judgements that are more reliable) against the drawbacks of labelling people or behaviours as 'abnormal'. In the next section, we turn to the process of diagnosis and concentrate on the interpretation and evaluation of human subjectivity as people bring their personal histories, feelings and meanings (personal narratives) to the clinic.

4.3   The process of diagnosis

The questions we will be exploring therefore are: how useful is diagnosing mental illness? And, what methodologies can be used to ensure that each individual is assessed in a valid and reliable way?

4.3.1 How can diagnoses be useful to those who are distressed, disabled or at risk?

To help you understand whether diagnoses may be useful, we turn to Samuel's very difficult circumstances (see Vignette 4.1), which you should read now.

Vignette 4.1 Samuel's bipolar disorder

Samuel is a 34-year-old telecommunications graduate who has managed an innovations unit at a top UK telecommunications company for the last 12 months. Despite being regarded by his peers as a rising star, Samuel has recently returned to live with his parents. Since his return Beth, his mother, has noticed that he hasn't been his usual self. He has slept very little and has worked non-stop to set up a company to produce a new generation of mobile phones that he says 'will scan barcodes and effectively double as a credit card' – the 'scanphone', as he calls it.

Three weeks ago, following a spell of overconfidence at the wheel, Samuel hit a car in heavy traffic and picked a fight with another driver, badly hurting his own wrist and face. He admitted to Beth that he had been drinking but only agreed to come to hospital two days later.

Usually a calm person, he kept shouting 'I am too busy!' and only the pain finally convinced him to have his wrist X-rayed. As he waited to be seen by the medical staff, Samuel became so talkative that he approached nearly everyone around him, and began telling them about his plans to attain fame and fortune. 'I am planning a commercial revolution!', he repeated, in a vibrant mood.

Beth has often been unable to locate him during office hours, but he has been seen drinking in the village where they live. Two weeks ago he said to his mother, 'They're trying to get me, I know they are because I'm sure they're taping the conversations I have in the office so they can steal my plans. I have had enough so I am going to resign'. To Beth's astonishment he added, 'Don't you worry, many investors want to back me up. The papers are already talking about me because they heard rumours about my scanphone'.

Meanwhile, although Samuel had contacted hundreds of telecommunications company directors worldwide, hoping to attract their interest and funding for his new product, he had only one reply from a start-up company in Malaysia, inviting him for a meeting. So he funded his trip to Kuala Lumpur. 'They understand I am a gifted innovator', he told his parents at the airport.

However, something changed upon Samuel's return from Malaysia. In stark contrast to his previous pattern of behaviour, he has told no one about the outcomes of his meeting and hasn't left his room since he arrived. Meanwhile, Beth reported that the changes in Samuel's behaviour started several months after his partner died in a car accident whilst he was at the wheel. They had to wait for nearly two hours before the rescue team finally cut them both out of the wreckage.

Although he asked to see his GP, it was only to request prolonged sick leave: 'I am not ready to return to work', he said. The GP referred Samuel to a mental health team (see Box 4.1) with the question: 'bipolar/ schizophrenia/PTSD?'

Post-traumatic stress disorder, PTSD, is an anxiety disorder that can develop after exposure to a terrifying event or ordeal in which grave physical harm occurred or was threatened.

More often than not, when someone is referred to a mental health clinician, he or she may feel confused and fearful about the future. Whereas Samuel felt elated before his trip to Malaysia, he now feels isolated, unappreciated and misunderstood. For someone in his situation, a diagnosis may be a welcome way to clarify that he is suffering from a recognised condition, as this may help him understand why certain symptoms are occurring, what is causing his unexplained behaviours, and reassure him that he will receive appropriate treatment.

There are four reasons why diagnoses are useful. Firstly, from the clinician's perspective, a correct diagnosis will enable the recommendation of a treatment that will have been previously tried and tested for a particular syndrome, enabling better quality care. Misdiagnosing Samuel would have significant consequences in terms of medication, for example. An appropriate treatment, on the other hand, will also increase Samuel's chance of returning to work, or any previous activity, and, hopefully, to a fulfilling life.

Secondly, diagnoses facilitate communication amongst clinicians and become a sort of shorthand to convey complex descriptions. Thirdly, diagnoses are crucial in enabling researchers to investigate what people with specific syndromes may have in common, both in terms of causes of the disorder (or **aetiology**) and treatment.

Finally, diagnoses are essential for the economics of mental health and third parties, such as medical insurance companies. Several crucial decisions are based on diagnostic criteria and insurance companies will not cover assessment and care costs unless the patient has a diagnosis and an indication for treatment.

- ■ Can you think of reasons why some people would not like being diagnosed with a mental health condition?

- □ Although some may feel that a diagnosis has helped them cope with uncertainty ('I am not alone'), others may find the situation uncomfortable, feeling that they are being pigeon-holed or stuck with a label, rather than seen as individuals with particular problems that they need help with. Unfortunately, mental illness still carries a stigma (or negative labelling) in many cultures, which may result in former friends and colleagues withdrawing from contact.

4.3.2 Psychological assessment: building a database

Figure 4.15 details the several steps involved in the process of diagnosis, beginning with psychological assessment (the heading of this section). You will be using the steps described in the left-hand side of Figure 4.15 as sub-headings to help you navigate through this section.

The primary purpose of a psychological assessment is to evaluate the person's beliefs, mental and emotional state, behaviours, personality characteristics (or traits), strengths and impairments. This information is essential so that judgements, diagnoses, predictions and treatment recommendations may be made. Also, in line with the biopsychosocial model (Engel, 1977), competent assessments should clarify the interpersonal and environmental factors that may have contributed to the problems and the difficulties that moved the person to seek help.

An accurate description of the person's problems, and an insider's view about the various factors that prolong them, will increase the validity of predictions of possible outcomes and help the clinician decide whether an intervention is needed – or not. Additionally, psychological testing can either support (or challenge) previous working diagnoses, as well as identify adjustments to treatment. In practice, clinicians generally base their assessment on a clinical interview, which sets the basic context for most other psychological assessments, as will be discussed next.

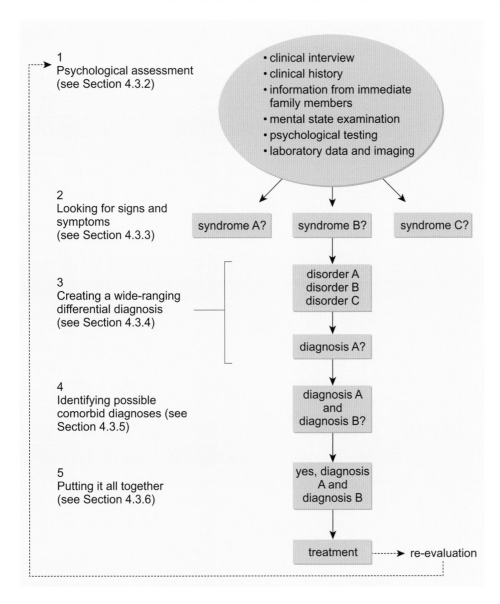

Figure 4.15 The process of diagnosis.

The clinical interview, clinical history and informants

A **clinical interview** is a conversation with an investigative purpose. As such, it requires a degree of structure designed to obtain information about the person's mental health symptoms, any relevant life events and, crucially, their perceptions about the current situation. Clinical interviews have, for these reasons, directed content. They also imply clear roles between the participants and take place at a definite time and place.

The ability to tap into an 'insider's perspective' requires considerable skill on the part of the clinician, including the ability to establish a rapport of trust with the person (Figure 4.16). For this, the clinician will need to convey to the interviewee that their feelings and attitudes are understood. The clinician ought to use open-ended rather than close-ended questions to extract more information, whilst using language that may easily be understood by the person. Successful interviewers are also good listeners and will allow the interviewee to use silence for reflection. They eliminate distractions, remain alert and focused, and are patient and open-minded.

Clinical history

The clinical interview usually begins with a **clinical history** where the clinician gathers specific information about the person's previous mental health history, including earlier manifestations of the current complaint, or other mental and emotional problems that may have required clinical attention, as these may guide the investigation of what is currently wrong. What were Samuel's immediate reasons for seeking help? When did the presenting complaint become a problem and who defined it as such?

Such questions aim at obtaining useful information for the formulation of a diagnosis and the selection of a treatment. You may recall, for example, that Samuel's current depression was preceded by a period of euphoria, mania and increased alcohol intake. Other important sources of information will include Samuel's family history of mental disorder and his medical background.

Put in a different way, the clinician will focus on any recent or long-standing key events (and issues) in Samuel's life, whilst evaluating their impact on his mental health. To evaluate whether the person's pattern of behaviours is abnormal (or clinically significant, which means they may be causing significant distress, disability or risk), the clinician will need to keep track of what has happened, when it happened, how often, for how long and how intense and how disabling the relevant behaviours may have been (see Section 4.1.1).

- How have Samuel's symptoms changed since the problems started?

- He had an acute episode of mania followed by deep depression and isolation that has made him unable to go to work.

Information from immediate family members

Samuel's mother reported that her mother had had a history of 'euphoric periods' with nearly no sleep and gambling losses. Because 'grandma' had not received treatment for mental health disorders, her 'episodes' had vanished from family conversations after one generation and Samuel was not aware of them. Yet, this information suggests a potential genetic explanation for his current condition.

Mental state examination

In contrast to the previous historical information, the **mental state examination** is a statement, or snapshot, of the patient's psychological symptoms at the time of the interview. During the mental state examination the clinician will attempt to elicit signs of mental disorder in an objective way, by evaluating the form and the content of the person's responses. In some cases, the clinician may suspect **malingering** (see Box 4.8). The form of a patient's thoughts may be delusional (delusions are false beliefs that are resistant to confrontation with actual facts), and the content of the delusions

Figure 4.16 Patient being interviewed by a clinical psychologist.

may concern beliefs about family or neighbours. Whilst conducting a mental state examination, the clinician will take into consideration the person's appearance (attire, cleanliness, posture and gait), behaviour (facial expression, cooperation or aggression, activity, agitation, level of arousal) and speech (form and pattern, volume and rate; is it coherent, logical, and congruent with questioning?).

Box 4.8 Malingering

A malingerer is someone who deliberately pretends to have an illness or disability in order to receive financial or other gain – or to avoid punishment or responsibility. This generally includes people who have committed a crime and want to make a legal defence based on a mental disorder, or have been ordered by the judicial system to be psychologically tested, evaluated and diagnosed; those who have been ordered by the judicial system to receive psychotherapy or are someone who is suing a third party on the grounds of psychological damages.

Clinicians are often aware of 'red alert' behaviours that signal potential malingering. Some examples include spotty amnesia (i.e. someone may claim to have forgotten personal information but can chat about current issues in the news), poor cooperation or extreme language to describe symptoms: for example, 'I lost 20 pounds in five days'.

Other relevant aspects include mood (apathetic, irritable, labile, optimistic or pessimistic, thoughts of suicide; do reported experience and observable mood agree?), thought (particular preoccupations, ideas and beliefs; are they rational, fixed or delusional? Do they concern the safety of the patient or other people?), perception (abnormalities including hallucinations, or illusory perceptions, occurring in any modality; i.e. auditory, visual, smell, taste, touch), intellect (is the patient able to function intellectually at the level expected from his or her history?) and insight (how does the patient explain or attribute his or her symptoms?).

Psychological testing, laboratory data, and neuroimaging

Individuals are different, so each psychological assessment will require the combination of several tests and techniques that are selected by the clinician according to the type of investigation being made. Although no particular assessment measure will be 'better' or more complete than others, the various techniques will complement each other and help provide a more comprehensive picture of the person. Tests will objectively quantify a subjective quality already detected by the clinician. So, for example, although the clinician may know that Samuel is currently depressed, he or she may want to quantify his level of depression and compare it to the general population, or the norm.

The choice of tests is vast, including evaluations of depression, personality disorders, or cognitive impairments, such as memory loss. Occasionally, some mental health patients will require neuroimaging results, although these cases tend to be related to accidents, neural disease (e.g. tumours or stroke) or dementia, a theme to which we will return in Book 4.

To illustrate the relevance of testing, we will concentrate on three examples: the Beck Depression Inventory (BDI-II) to evaluate depression, the Impact of Event Scale (IES-R) to evaluate distress in response to trauma, and the Minnesota Multiphasic Personality Inventory (MMPI-2) to evaluate personality disorders. Note that the choice of tests varies from country to country.

Beck Depression Inventory-II (BDI-II)

The BDI-II (1996) is a widely used 21-question multiple-choice self-report inventory for measuring the severity of depression (Box 4.9) that Samuel is likely to have completed during his assessment so that a baseline may be established. A baseline is an initial evaluation to which the effectiveness of treatment may be compared whilst trying to establish how much change has occurred. In its current version, the questionnaire includes items relating to symptoms of depression such as hopelessness and irritability, cognitions such as guilt or feelings of being punished, as well as physical symptoms such as fatigue, weight loss and lack of interest in sex (Beck, 2006). The manual of the BDI-II recommends the following cut score guidelines, with the recommendation that thresholds be adjusted based on the characteristics of the sample, and the purpose for use of the inventory: total score of 0–13 is considered minimal, 14–19 is mild, 20–28 is moderate, and 29–63 is severe depression.

Box 4.9 Sample items from the Beck Depression Inventory (1996 edition) (BDI-II)

Unhappiness
   0 I do not feel unhappy.
   1 I feel unhappy.
   2 I am unhappy.
   3 I am so unhappy that I can't stand it.
Changes in activity level
   0   I have not experienced any change in activity level.
  1a I am somewhat more active than usual.
  1b I am somewhat less active than usual.
  2a I am a lot more active than usual.
  2b I am a lot less active than usual.
  3a I am not active most of the day.
  3b I am active all day.

The BDI is widely used in different countries as an assessment tool by health care professionals and researchers in a variety of settings to monitor changes in depressive states over time. It is also used to provide a measure for judging improvement and the effectiveness of treatment methods. The BDI has been translated into various European languages, Arabic, Chinese, Japanese and Farsi (Persian) amongst many others.

■   The inventory is completed by the person being assessed. What limitations is this likely to impose on its validity?

☐   As in other self-report inventories, the scores can be easily exaggerated (or minimised) by the person completing them.

The BDI has some limitations. For instance, the way the instrument is administered and where it is administered can have an effect on the final score. Think, for example, of the different effects of completing the questionnaire either in front of clinical staff or at home. Also, in participants with concomitant physical illness, the BDI's inclusion of some physical items (such as activity level; see Box 4.9) may artificially inflate scores due to associated symptoms of the illness, rather than the depression itself. Finally, although it was designed as a screening device rather than a diagnostic tool, the BDI is sometimes used by health care providers to reach a quick diagnosis (Hersen et al., 2007), which may bias the results.

The Impact of Event Scale – Revised (IES-R)

The IES-R is a 22-item easy-to-administer questionnaire used to evaluate the degree of distress a patient may feel in response to trauma. Samuel may suffer debilitating physical and psychological symptoms without recognising that they are a response to a traumatic event (the accident in which his partner died). Older adults in particular may be reluctant to admit to experiencing such symptoms as they may fear being seen as weak or not in control of their lives.

Samuel will be asked to indicate the degree of his distress for each of 22 symptoms according to a five-point scale: 0 indicates that the symptom occurs 'not at all'; 1, 'a little bit'; 2, 'moderately'; 3, 'quite a bit'; and 4, 'extremely'.

The questionnaire is based on three clusters of symptoms identified in the DSM-IV-TR as indicators of post-traumatic stress disorder (PTSD): intrusion (e.g. 'I thought about it when I didn't mean to'), avoidance (e.g. 'I tried not to talk about it') and hyperarousal (e.g. 'I was jumpy and easily startled').

The IES-R relies on a patient's own report of symptoms and is used to gauge response no sooner than two weeks after a traumatic event. Although it was not intended as a diagnostic or screening tool for PTSD, it is commonly employed as a screening measure to assess the presence and severity of PTSD symptoms, showing good validity and reliability (Rash et al., 2008). The questionnaire is short, easily administered and scored, and can be used repeatedly to assess progress or to evaluate recovery.

The Minnesota multiphasic personality inventory-2 (MMPI-2)

The MMPI-2 (1989) is, perhaps, the most frequently used personality test in mental health, used by trained clinicians to assist in the identification of personality disorders (also for research). The test has three validity scales (you may like to revisit the concept of validity in Section 4.2.4) that inform whether the patient is lying (L), malingering (F) or manipulating the responses to appear in a better light (K). The MMPI-2 also includes 13 strictly clinical scales (see the key at the bottom of the graph presented in Figure 4.17).

Traditionally, clinicians were discouraged by the legendary long time it took to administer and score the MMPI-2. However, modern software has solved that problem.

The data from the patient's answers to 567 items in the various scales provide a profile that can be used in conjunction with a clinician's assessment to help assess personality functioning, coping style and potential obstacles to treatment. Figure 4.17 compares pre- (i.e. baseline) and post-treatment results after nineteen 30-minute neurofeedback (Box 4.10) sessions for a single patient with depression (Hammond, 2005). Note that the yellow band in Figure 4.17 indicates the normality range.

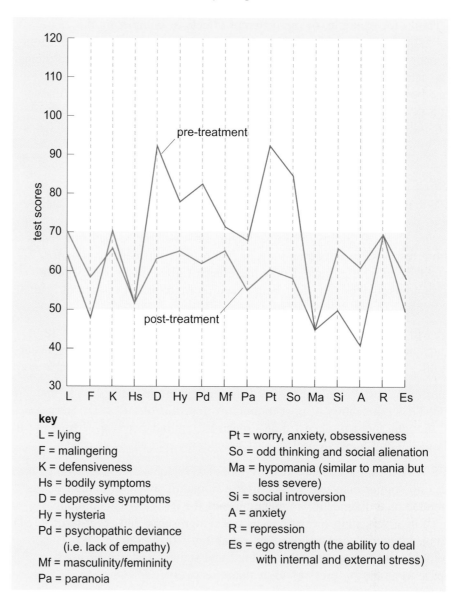

Figure 4.17 MMPI-2 results before and after 19 neurofeedback sessions for depression.

■   What do you notice about Figure 4.17?

☐   The values of nearly all scales have been reduced following treatment. For example, the patient is now less depressed (D), worried (Pt) and anxious (A).

Box 4.10 What is neurofeedback?

Neurofeedback, or neurotherapy, is a technique that uses electroencephalography (EEG) to train the brain to regulate functions of the body and mind, by providing a signal that informs individuals about their brain activity. As discussed in Section 2.2.2, an EEG is the recording of electrical activity along the scalp produced by the firing of groups of neurons as they communicate with each other.

One of the technique's strengths is that it draws upon the brain's own ability to learn and adapt. Sensors are placed on the scalp to measure electrical activity and the client is taught to modify their cognitive responses, which translates into altered behaviour (Figure 4.18).

For the purposes of neurofeedback, the raw EEG measurements can be analysed through sophisticated software and the data transformed into quantitative EEG (or QEEG). The data can then be displayed using colour-coded frequency scales (Figure 4.19). Over several sessions, the person is given information about how his or her brain is functioning, which can be used to learn to modify and control their own brain waves.

Neurofeedback is a safe and non-invasive technique that, rather than trying to affect the body from the outside, makes certain patterns of the brain's operation visible to the conscious mind.

Figure 4.18 A client with depression during a neurofeedback session.

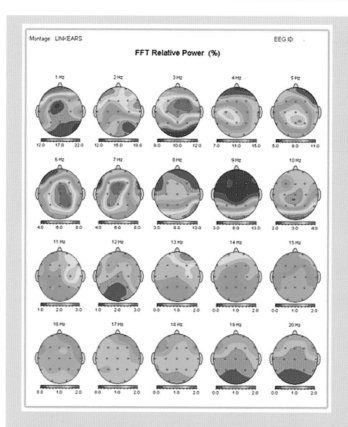

Figure 4.19 Typical QEEG imaging display showing different wave frequency distributions in the brain according to a colour-coded scale. Red and blue indicate relatively high and low activity, respectively, at each frequency from 1 Hz up to 20 Hz.

Figure 4.20 Signs can be powerful indicators of mental health problems.

4.3.3 Looking for signs and symptoms

As the assessment progresses, the clinician will investigate the nature, duration and severity of the patient's signs and symptoms, and evaluate whether Samuel's behaviour, for example, fits either syndrome A, B or C (see Figure 4.15). The distinction between signs and symptoms is crucial to help the clinician focus and discriminate the relevance and meaning of each of these sources of information. It will also help you understand what clinicians will be looking for whilst they take a clinical history, so it is worth expanding on these notions.

To remind you, 'signs' are what the clinician sees, symptoms are what the person reports experiencing. As such, a sign is an objective indication of mental disease that may be noticed by others (Figure 4.20). Comparatively, mental health does not have as many signs as those found in physical health. However, some very important ones include: weeping, sighing, pacing, weight loss, slumped posture, poor hygiene and tattered clothing. On the other hand, a symptom is a subjective (and uncomfortable) sensation that indicates a change in the functioning of the person. A headache, sadness and depression or the feeling of a 'heavy chest' are examples of symptoms that a patient might report, but the clinician cannot observe. Let's return to Samuel's case to see if you can detect such differences (see Vignette 4.2).

Vignette 4.2 More about Samuel's signs and symptoms

You may recall that Samuel had been referred to a clinical psychologist for further investigation. During his clinical interview he sat with slumped shoulders and was moderately uncooperative; that is, he stayed either silent or monosyllabic for most of the interview except when he felt the need to stress that he was not depressed. He gets very angry when anyone suggests that he may be depressed. He also looked 'scruffy' and was, at times, tearful. His only complaints were that he could not sleep and had headaches 'most of the time'. He also eats very little and is not seeing friends or colleagues. He currently spends most of his days playing violent computer games through the night and sleeps during the day.

Activity 4.3 Can you distinguish between Samuel's signs and symptoms?

(LO 4.4) Allow 10 minutes

List Samuel's signs and symptoms (Vignettes 4.1 and 4.2), taking care to distinguish between these two categories. Compare your lists with the one given at the end of the chapter.

Patients are often unaware of signs and do not usually complain about them; instead they carry them around as silent indicators that something is not right. It is unlikely, for example, that Samuel should say 'look how scruffy I am these days' or 'my shoulders have slumped', although he says he has headaches (symptom) but feels no depression (symptom). Yet, his slumped posture, scruffy looks and watery eyes (all important signs) tell a different story.

We now turn to Stacey's case (Vignette 4.3). Like John (in Chapter 1), she suffers from OCD but, in this case, we see how the disorder has affected her life in a slightly different way.

Vignette 4.3 Stacey's OCD

Stacey lives in Liverpool (UK) and was referred for help by her GP. The referral note was very brief, indicating a pronounced hand-washing compulsion that was beginning to affect her work and studies. She works as a cleaner at a hospital and is training to become a cook at her local

Hyperhidrosis is a condition characterised by abnormally increased perspiration. People with hyperhidrosis sweat profusely from the hands, feet and armpits. The condition affects nearly 3% of the population of the UK.

college. Stacey is a 23-year-old woman who portrayed herself as well adjusted throughout the clinical interview. She smiled frequently and appeared to be emotionally well adjusted. There was no hint of depression.

Stacey was the eldest of three children. Her father died when she was six, and her mother is a school dinner lady. Since childhood (the age of six or seven) she suffered from extreme '**hyperhidrosis**', which left her with hands dripping wet for much of the time. She was very embarrassed by this unusual condition and would hide her hands most of the time, especially when expected to shake hands with someone. Any attempt to write at school was likely to result in soaking wet paper, and she recalled submitting exam scripts that were barely readable due to sweat impregnation. Handling paper money was another very embarrassing situation.

Consequently, she has developed an irresistible urge (or a compulsion) to wash her hands often several times within an hour. If she is at work, she says she must also go through the ritual of carefully washing the basin and taps with a wet tissue and rubber gloves – which she carries in her handbag. If she goes out with friends, she must ensure that there is a toilet somewhere near so she may wash her hands. This compulsion now extends somewhat to other cleaning activities. For example, she frequently spends 30 minutes in the shower, and this can extend to 45 minutes. However, she says that her activities in the shower do not include specific rituals.

The compulsive hand-washing is related to intrusive thoughts about dirt and contamination, which are somewhat obsessive but not entirely unnecessary, given her work. For example, she is afraid that her hands may have come into contact with sources of infection and that she may contaminate herself or others. Working in the hospital, she is frequently exposed to possible contact with blood and she is very worried by the possibility of contracting hepatitis or some other serious disease; despite wearing gloves. She spoke of her profound distress, for example, when asked to dispose of the dressings of patients who were HIV-positive.

There are other related minor signs. For example, she tends to hoard things and procrastinates about unpacking luggage, so that some luggage from her last holiday, nearly a year ago, remains unpacked. She also has the habit of plucking her eyebrows, which has left visible marks.

Stacey also says she feels somewhat overweight although this didn't appear to be the case. She believes that her self-consciousness about her body is responsible for the fact that she has not had a serious relationship. She does, however, have many friends and enjoys an active social life. She drinks, but not excessively, and does not smoke. She says that she doesn't feel anxious but also admits that she is very good at hiding her symptoms. However, other people, including colleagues and her family, have noticed and made comments and she is sure if she had a partner her problems would be very apparent. She feels that the OCD is a significant problem and does become depressed about it at times. She says that her intrusive thoughts have been worse since she started failing in her studies at college.

■   Stacey *says* she does not feel anxious. What are her detectable signs of anxiety?

☐   Her signs of anxiety include plucking her eyebrows to the point of leaving visible marks, and increased washing rituals in response to more intrusive negative thoughts.

Here are some important points to bear in mind about symptoms and signs. First, they can, sometimes, be confused. Stacey's sweaty hands are both a sign and a symptom because they are a complaint that can also be seen by a third person. Second, symptoms and signs can be context-dependent. For example, reports of delusion (symptom) by some participants in the 100-mile endurance run may only be a biological phenomenon caused by the tremendous effort and physical pain they must endure during the two-day race. Also, someone breaking down in tears (sign) during dinner with a friend may not mean they are depressed and in need of treatment: they could be only reacting to appalling news about the death of a loved one.

■   How are signs and symptoms useful to the clinician?

☐   They are useful in two ways. On the one hand, their sudden manifestation and level of intensity indicate, rather like alarm bells, that something is not right. Secondly, signs and symptoms help the clinician formulate an appropriate diagnosis. For example, a pattern of repeated public intoxication suggests alcohol dependence. Sadness and isolation suggest depression.

■   How does context help the interpretation of Stacey's symptoms?

☐   From an early age she learned that washing her hands, and then drying them thoroughly, brought some relief and it's easy to recognise this as generating a behaviour pattern that would later constitute hand-washing OCD. Also, she's afraid of viral contamination but she works in a hospital unit with a high risk of contamination.

As pointed out by Kraepelin in the 19th century, one of the 'headaches' of diagnosing is that different mental illnesses are likely to have some symptoms in common. So, to reduce uncertainty, clinicians ask 'what is the difference' between the several candidate syndromes and which of them could best explain Samuel's and Stacey's patterns of behaviour? We turn to these questions in the next section on differential diagnosis.

Activity 4.4 The experience of being diagnosed

(LO 4.3) Allow 30 minutes

Now would be an ideal time to go to the multimedia map and listen to the interviews with people who have experienced the process of diagnosis. Then follow the instructions in the activity.

4.3.4 Creating a wide-ranging differential diagnosis

The assumption that 'significant recent substance abuse' refers exclusively to alcohol or street drugs misuse is often incorrect. Both prescription and over-the-counter medications can also cause mental symptoms.

Differential diagnosis is the process of weighing the probability of one disorder versus that of other disorders possibly accounting for a patient's illness. At this stage, the clinician will be discriminating between disorders A, B and C to arrive at a diagnosis (see Figure 4.15). Differential diagnosis is part of everyday life experience, albeit in an informal way. Say one Saturday morning you wake up feeling sick and shivering. At some point you may start asking yourself about the causes of your state of nausea and diarrhoea. Could it have been the bottle of red wine or was it that rather large chocolate mousse you mixed with it? Maybe it was the wine and the chocolate plus the brandy you had next? But then you may also remember: no, not the wine, nor the mixture with the mousse plus the brandy; you know you can cope with that. So, taking into account the diarrhoea (the novelty), you conclude that some bug may have taken over your digestive system and the odds are that you may have eaten contaminated food.

Samuel, for example, has displayed a range of symptoms including overconfidence, euphoria (intense, usually exaggerated, mental or emotional state of elation and well-being), little sleep, persecutory delusions (the belief that someone is trying to harm him), aggressiveness and grandiose delusions (the belief that he is famous, important and powerful). As we concentrate for a moment on Samuel's delusions, note that they are common to at least three syndromes: substance abuse disorder, bipolar disorder and schizophrenia (see Figure 4.21a).

In some cases, patients with multiple sclerosis, brain tumour or hypothyroidism could also show mood disorders, such as bipolar disorders. These would have been diagnosed using the DSM's Axis III, where the clinician would note any acute medical condition that may be affecting the person, and could later be ruled out through a neurological examination and hormonal tests (e.g. to assess the thyroid). Let's assume that this has been done in Samuel's case.

A second possibility could be a substance-induced mood disorder. We know that Samuel wasn't medicated nor consumed drugs. Yet he has a recent history of excessive alcohol consumption, which could account for some of his recent behaviour, including antisocial behaviour, although substance abuse on its own could not explain all his symptoms and signs. A third possibility could be a psychotic disorder such as schizophrenia. However, delusions were not Samuel's 'dominant' symptom, and they disappeared after the trip to Malaysia.

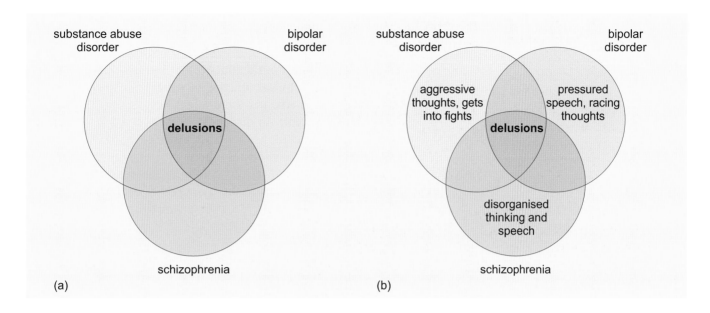

Figure 4.21 Differential diagnosis. (a) The same symptom may be shared by several disorders. (b) Differences in other characteristics (e.g. speech) may help to make a differential diagnosis.

Also, the onset of schizophrenia usually happens during the late teens or early adulthood – Samuel is 34, has no prior delusional behaviour and no family history of schizophrenia. Bipolar disorder, of which Samuel does have a family history, seems a better explanation for his current behaviour.

■ What else in Figure 4.21b can help to make finer discriminations that may lead to a differential diagnosis?

▢ It is possible to discriminate differences in speech, for example. Samuel has shown pressured speech and racing thoughts (typical of bipolar disorder) but no disorganised thinking (typical of schizophrenia). Also, the content of his thoughts were not predominantly aggressive (as in substance abuse disorder), although we know that he got into a fight (once) over a small traffic incident.

Having made a differential diagnosis, the clinician then asks: could this patient have any other mental illness? This issue is explored in the next section.

4.3.5 Identifying possible comorbid diagnoses

The term **comorbidity** was introduced in the 1970s (Feinstein, 1970) to refer to the presence of more than one diagnosis in an individual at the same time. As an epidemiologist, Feinstein was referring to physical disorders whilst making the point that undetected comorbidities, or *hidden disorders*, could alter the clinical course of patients with the same diagnosis, by affecting the time of detection, prognostic anticipations, therapeutic selection, and post-therapeutic outcome of the disease. As such, the possibility of hidden disorders should be investigated. This concept has been applied in mental health contexts where, after the first diagnosis, and whilst looking for an additional clinical entity, the clinician asks, 'Is there anything *else* affecting this patient?'

The above, however, reflects a clear-cut definition that has become problematic in today's everyday clinical practice in mental health settings, where clinicians are interested in whether there might be additional *mental health* disorders in the same patient. As discussed in Section 4.2.3, one of the difficulties is that the diagnostic classification systems (e.g. the DSM) have meanwhile changed and now list considerably more categories in comparison to only 30 years ago. Based on this, Maj (2005) and others have argued that comorbidity has become a 'by-product' of the more recent diagnostic systems (i.e. the DSM and the ICD) that currently include *too many* minute distinctions based on small differences in symptoms. For example, a person with antisocial behaviour personality disorder (ASPD, Axis II) is also highly likely to meet diagnostic criteria for substance abuse. However, the DSM-IV-TR diagnoses ASPD and substance abuse as separate disorders, which automatically creates a comorbidity.

Evidence that nearly half (or 45%) of the patients who have been diagnosed with a disorder will meet the criteria for at least a second diagnosis (Kessler et al., 2005) clearly suggests that comorbidity, arising from the use of DSM or ICD symptom-based criteria, has become the norm rather than the exception. In fact, only 26% of the participants in a previous survey by the same authors could be said to be free of a concomitant, or comorbid, mental disorder (Kessler et al., 1994).

But how does this apply to the cases of Samuel and Stacey? You may recall that Samuel was diagnosed with bipolar disorder, probably resulting from a combination of factors including his family history. Concomitantly, he *also* met the diagnostic criteria for PTSD, following a traumatic car accident where his partner died. Thus, Samuel's bipolar and the PTSD would be described as comorbid. Stacey, on the other hand, has OCD and has also shown signs of anxiety. However, because these do not meet the DSM's criteria for a separate diagnosis for generalised anxiety disorder (or GAD, also discussed in Book 2, Section 1.4.4), they are not described as comorbid (see also Book 2, Section 1.5.2 for how DSM criteria affect diagnosis in cases of depression and anxiety).

■ What are the current main difficulties associated with the identification of comorbidities?

□ It is difficult to establish whether concomitant diagnoses actually reflect the presence of *separate* mental disorders or refer to *multiple manifestations* of a single disorder.

■ Can you think of a factor that bears direct relation to the current difficulties associated with the identification of comorbidities?

□ Yes: the recent proliferation of diagnostic categories in the DSM, for example. They include too many minute distinctions based on small differences in symptoms and at times lose sight of the person as a whole. This means that comorbidity could, in many cases, simply reflect the current inability to supply a single diagnosis that accounts for and relates all symptoms.

4.3.6 Putting it all together: the case formulation

During the last step of the process, the clinician will gather all relevant information and attempt to come up with a **case formulation** that presents a theory, or a conceptualisation, of the patient's current state. In short, what does the information provided by the clinical interview and assessment mean, and how does it improve the clinician's understanding about the patient? This information is usually returned to the GP who had referred the patient to the mental health specialist asking for a specific question to be investigated (see Vignette 4.1).

Vignette 4.3 (Stacey's OCD) provides an example of a case formulation.

Integrating the biological, psychological and social factors in assessment and diagnosis

The case formulation includes a hypothesis about the causes, triggers, and maintaining influences of a person's biological functioning (major illnesses, possible genetic vulnerability to mental illness, brain functioning), psychological functioning (personality, coping skills, intellectual strengths, symptoms) and social functioning (support networks, work relationships, social skills), as shown in Figure 4.22. It also elaborates on how strengths and impairments in one area may be influencing functioning in another area, highlighting how these complex interactions will be highly specific to individual circumstances, although two different patients may have the same diagnosis.

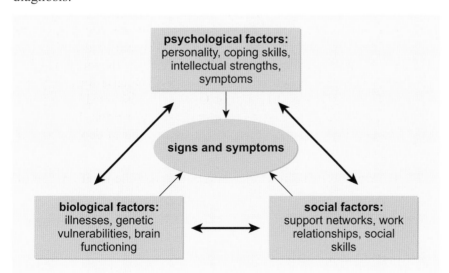

Figure 4.22 The integration of biological, psychological and social factors in assessment and diagnosis.

A case formulation helps organise often intricate and contradictory information about a person, highlighting the dominant patterns that may explain their situation. Ideally, it should also serve as a blueprint (or framework) to guide treatment, establishing tangible markers to evaluate change, and a structure to enable the clinician to follow the patient up. The case formulation is particularly useful in conveying essential information: for example, when reporting the patient to another specialist or back to the family doctor, after a psychological assessment. A similar methodology, known as case study, is also used in mental health research (see Box 4.11).

Phineas Gage was a railway construction worker until 1848 when an accidental explosion drove an iron bar through his skull destroying part of his left frontal cortex. He survived the accident albeit with a visibly altered personality and changed emotional behaviour.

Box 4.11 Research Methods: Case studies

Case studies use a variety of techniques, such as clinical interviews, direct observation, psychological tests and the review of documents, to obtain an in-depth analysis of a subject. They are most often used in clinical research to illustrate specific situations or describe rare events and conditions, and the results can sometimes contradict well-established principles in the field of psychology. For example, the famous Phineas Gage case study showed that the frontal cortex processed emotional information, whereas up to that point it was believed that the emotions were processed exclusively in the deeper areas of the brain (Damasio, 1996). In a case study, nearly every aspect of the subject's life and history is analysed to seek patterns and causes for behaviour. The hope is that learning gained from studying one case can provide insight into many others.

The main advantage of case studies is that they can provide very detailed information and insight into the experiences of a particular individual or group of individuals. Case studies can be used to develop hypotheses and to provide possible avenues for future investigations. Further, the results of a case study can often disprove a hypothesis, leading to a re-evaluation of existing ideas. For these reasons, case studies play an important role in mental health research and provide a richness of information that cannot be obtained by larger scale studies.

A potential disadvantage of case studies, however, is that the results cannot be generalised to a whole population. The information recorded may be unique to a particular individual at a particular point in time. Also, the nature of the recording methods is such that there may be potential for bias or subjectivity on the part of the investigator, which may impact on the reliability of the results.

The research question and methods of data collection used in a case study must be carefully designed to ensure validity. Subjects can be chosen from within a defined context in order to answer certain questions: for example, researchers may want to explore mental health problems in people with a particular background or occupation. Sometimes unique or atypical subjects are selected for case studies. In other words, subjects are not usually chosen at random as they would be for an experimental study. The data obtained from case studies can be either quantitative, qualitative or both, but the emphasis tends to be on qualitative findings.

Re-evaluation

Diagnoses need adjustments because clinicians sometimes get it wrong (see Section 4.2.6), patient's symptoms (and signs) change or new data emerge. For example, an uncooperative patient such as Samuel may omit to mention his earlier symptoms of mania, which may lead the clinician to think that he is simply depressed (one of the phases of bipolar disorder). As soon as the manic phase begins, a new assessment and diagnosis will be needed. Also, despite the information collected during the assessment, a diagnosis may still leave some symptoms unexplained, in which case it is important to evaluate whether the known symptoms are responding to treatment. Finally, family history reports may only be available months later, which can produce further information that may lead to the revision of a previous diagnosis.

Activity 4.5 What have you learned about diagnosing mental health?

(LO 4.3) Allow 15 minutes

In Activity 4.1 (end of Section 4.1.2) you were asked to make some notes about how a person might feel about receiving a diagnosis of a mental illness and the possible advantages and disadvantages of receiving such a diagnosis. Return now to those notes and examine whether your perception about each of the issues you listed has changed (i.e. what do you know now that you didn't know then?) Summarise your findings in a few sentences.

4.4 Final word

This chapter has described the processes and methodologies involved in the assessment and diagnosis of people with mental illnesses. It initially discussed the 'logic' behind the current diagnostic categories, focusing on how tools such as the DSM (or the ICD) have increased the validity and reliability of diagnostic judgements made by clinicians in the last 40 years (as well as increasing the quality of epidemiological research into the causes of mental disorders). The chapter also highlighted potential diagnostic pitfalls, providing evidence that the clinical interpretation of individual signs, symptoms and syndromes may still be influenced by factors such as context, expectations, source credibility and cultural background. Diagnosing remains a difficult endeavour and sometimes a satisfactory diagnosis is difficult to reach, causing frustration in both the patients and their clinicians. Having said the above, the third part of the chapter then detailed the methodologies used to ensure as much objectivity as possible whilst assessing and diagnosing mental disorders. These include a good (i.e. careful and systematic) clinical history, a mental state examination, a study of the patient's signs and symptoms, and the use of psychological tests to quantify any emergent impairments. However, before a competent diagnosis may be reached the clinician must also exclude competing explanations for the disorder (differential diagnosis) and identify possible comorbidities. The process ends with a case formulation, which organises the essential findings within a biopsychosocial framework, whilst taking into consideration any requests specified in the referral request (usually by a GP or a court).

4.5 Summary of Chapter 4

- Mental illness is generally defined as an experiential and behavioural pattern causing significant psychological suffering, distress or disability that may represent potential risk to the self or others.

- Diagnosis is the process used to determine whether a person's signs and symptoms fit a particular syndrome in a way that is causing them significant distress, disability and (or) risk.

- Assessment is the series of steps and methods used to gather and evaluate relevant information about a patient, so that a diagnosis may be formulated and an appropriate treatment may be recommended. Cases sent to a specialist for further investigation (usually by a GP) are called referrals.

- Diagnostic systems for mental illness have changed considerably since the initial work of Kraepelin, at the end of the 19th century. Currently two systems are used in many countries around the world: the DSM-IV-TR, published by the American Psychiatric Association, and the ICD-10, published by the World Health Organization.

- The DSM-IV-TR includes nearly 300 different diagnostic categories for mental illness and one of its central features is the presentation of explicit rules for diagnosis. Such clarity has improved the reliability of the DSM, whilst providing a systematic foundation to investigate whether each diagnosis is valid.

- One of the advantages of recent editions of the DSM is that, through the five axes, the system guides clinicians to be sensitive to the role of biopsychosocial factors whilst diagnosing mental illness. In practice, however, the majority of clinicians (worldwide) tend to focus on Axes I and II.

- Despite many revisions of the DSM and the ICD, diagnosing requires clinical interpretation, which may limit the validity and reliability of diagnoses. Although diagnoses are seen as fundamental for treating and researching mental health illnesses, several studies have highlighted potential pitfalls of diagnosing mental illness.

- The evidence suggests that clinical interpretations may, in many cases, still be influenced by factors such as context, expectations, source credibility and cultural background.

- Diagnoses provide the first step in the discrimination of the causes of signs and symptoms and are, for this reason, the initial step in planning treatment. Because mental disorders are diagnosed on the basis of a clinical history, signs and symptoms, clinical interviews are used to make diagnoses.

- Signs and symptoms guide clinicians towards specific diagnoses. Clinicians use diagnostic information to choose adequate treatments, to communicate easily with colleagues, and do research. But the implications of diagnosing do not end in the clinic, as medical insurance companies will only accept to cover the costs of assessment and care based on diagnostic information.

- The diagnosis of mental disorders must rest with the patients' reports of the intensity and duration of signs and symptoms from their psychological assessment and testing, and clinician observation of their behaviour including a mental state examination. These clues are grouped together by the clinician into recognisable patterns known as syndromes. When the syndrome fits the criteria for a diagnosis (and causes significant distress, disability or risk), it constitutes a mental disorder.

- Other important steps of the process of diagnosis include the creation of a wide-ranging differential diagnosis and the identification of possible comorbid diagnoses. The case formulation organises the essential findings, taking into consideration any requests specified in the referral request.

4.6 Learning outcomes

LO 4.1 Understand the impact of the biomedical and the biopsychosocial models in the classification of mental health disorders. (KU1, KU2, CS3)

LO 4.2 Identify and distinguish issues of reliability and validity in diagnosis and assessment of mental health conditions. (KU1, KU5, CS1, CS4)

LO 4.3 Comment on the usefulness and potential dangers of diagnosing mental health problems. (KU3, KU4, CS1, CS2, CS4)

LO 4.4 Distinguish between signs and symptoms. (KU1, KU4, KU5, CS1, CS2, CS4)

LO 4.5 Distinguish between 'differential diagnosis' and 'comorbidity'. (KU1, KU4, KU5, CS1, CS2)

LO 4.6 Show that you understand the importance of the case formulation (KU1, KU3, KU4, KU5, CS1, CS2, CS5).

4.7 Self-assessment questions

SAQ 4.1 (LO 4.1)

How has mental health care evolved from the biomedical to the biopsychosocial model?

SAQ 4.2 (LO 4.2)

Why is validity such a complex issue in mental health assessment?

SAQ 4.3 (LO 4.3)

List the pros and cons of diagnosing mental illness.

SAQ 4.4 (LO 4.4)

What are the differences between signs and symptoms?

SAQ 4.5 (LO 4.5)

Why should the identification of possible comorbidities come after (and not before) a differential diagnosis?

SAQ 4.6 (LO 4.6)

Explain what a case formulation is and how it is used in the diagnosis and treatment of mental health illnesses.

Answers and comments

Answers to SAQs

SAQ 1.1

A subjective measure is the fear levels expressed by Helen on confronting the phobic situation. Objectively, the magnitude of fear can be measured by the time spent avoiding the situation (i.e. length of time between excursions outside). Recovery can be measured by a decline in reported intensity of fear by the individual (subjective) and an increase in time spent outdoors (objective).

SAQ 1.2

A reductionist approach would usually try to explain the mental events in terms of events in Neha's brain (though someone might see them simply in terms of social context). Caution might be needed so as not to see an account in terms of the brain as providing a superior position and thereby missing important social and psychological interventions. A biopsychosocial perspective would consider Neha's social context (e.g. social isolation), her psychological state (e.g. low mood and black thoughts) and the biology of her brain. It would consider all of these to be determinants of her ill-health and would see the interdependence between them.

SAQ 1.3

She might be lowering José's anxiety immediately after the checking and hence increasing the chance that it will be repeated. She is preventing him from learning that he could perform just one check and still be secure.

SAQ 2.1

Activity within the brain (nervous system) influences the secretion of hormones (endocrine system) and hormones influence the activity of regions of the brain.

SAQ 2.2

There is a relatively high activation of the right prefrontal cortex of people as they confront the fear-evoking situation. Successful treatment would be expected to be associated with a shift of activity towards the left PFC and changes in the activity of the autonomic nervous system.

SAQ 2.3

The correct answer is (c).

SAQ 2.4

(a) It is an inhibitory synapse because the natural neurotransmitter eliminates the activity in neuron 2. (b) The substance is an antagonist to the natural neurotransmitter as it restores the activity in neuron 2.

SAQ 2.5

Jim showed excessive activity in the branch of the ANS that reacts to emergencies, triggered by hostile thoughts and emotion. If Jim can replace the hostile thoughts by more benign ones, this should lift the activation of the emergency reaction. In turn, this should lower the degree to which metabolic fuels are mobilised throughout his body.

SAQ 3.1

The emotion and mood are that of relaxation, which is associated with the behaviour of resting. There is a diversion of blood away from the muscles that control the limbs and towards the gut. This is a time when there are not demands placed on the skeletal muscles for action and hence a good time for digestion to occur.

SAQ 3.2

The appropriate treatment would decrease activity in the sympathetic branch of the ANS or increase activity in the sympathetic branch, so (b) and (c) are correct.

SAQ 3.3

A time of exertion is a time of increased activity of the sympathetic branch of the ANS with an increased release of noradrenalin into the bloodstream. To attribute noradrenalin a role in the runner's high, investigators would need further evidence. For example, increased levels in the brain would need to be detected with some relationship observed between the level of noradrenalin and the strength of the 'high'.

SAQ 3.4

Behaviourally, oxytocin promotes contact-making, bonding, calming and trust. In terms of physiology, it also promotes calming by activating the parasympathetic branch of the ANS and suppressing the secretion of ACTH and, thereby, the secretion of cortisol. As a hormone, it is involved in maternal behaviour.

SAQ 3.5

(a) Meditation is experienced by the meditator as an altered state of consciousness. According to the assumptions of Chapter 1, this would correspond to an altered activity pattern within the brain, as compared to when the person is not meditating.

(b) The *brain* consists of billions of *cells*, some of these being termed *neurons*. Some neurons employ *serotonin* as their neurotransmitter.

Meditation would consist of patterns of altered activity within a population of neurons, some of which employ serotonin and are excited at this time.

SAQ 4.1

The initial diagnostic classification systems were based on the biomedical model, which focused on disease more than the whole person, and on the discrimination between what are 'normal' and 'pathological' symptoms (and the inherent judgements about the boundary between them). Currently, mental disorders are better understood in terms of a combination of biological, psychological and social factors, rather than purely in biological terms. The DSM, for example, currently invites clinicians to evaluate patients along five axes contemplating the biopsychosocial model. The current model relies on the understanding of the person's signs and symptoms in context, further considering their experiences, perceptions and beliefs about their situation.

SAQ 4.2

Because mental health assessment involves the measurement of subjective individual traits that cannot be measured directly and objectively – trauma, for example. Instead, the measurement must rely on the interpretation of a test thought to measure trauma. The problem is that people change constantly. They also perceive their own psychological states differently. Finally, any concepts and definitions about trauma are bound to change as well.

SAQ 4.3

Pros: a correct diagnosis will enable the recommendation of a previously tried and tested treatment for a particular syndrome, enabling better quality care. Diagnoses facilitate communication amongst clinicians and become a sort of shorthand to convey complex descriptions. They also support epidemiological investigations about the causes of mental illnesses. Finally, diagnoses are essential for the economics of mental health and third parties (e.g. medical insurance companies) and underpin many judicial decisions.

Cons: despite tangible improvements in the DSM (and the ICD), which have led to clearer descriptions of the different diagnostic categories, diagnosing still relies a great deal on the clinical interpretation of the patient's symptoms and their life situations. The evidence suggests that these interpretations may be influenced by factors such as context, clinician expectations, source credibility and cultural background. Unfortunately, diagnosing still carries a stigma associated with instability, unreliability and vulnerability that has proven difficult to shake.

SAQ 4.4

A sign is an objective indication of mental disease that may be noticed by others. For example, weeping, weight loss, slumped posture and poor personal hygiene. A symptom is a subjective (and uncomfortable) sensation that indicates a change in the functioning of the person. Although a patient may report symptoms, the clinician cannot observe them. For instance, headaches, sadness and the feeling of a 'heavy chest' are all examples of symptoms. In some cases, however, signs and symptoms may overlap. For example, Stacey's hyperhidrosis is both a sign and a symptom because the clinician can also see what she reports as 'sweaty hands', objectively.

SAQ 4.5

Differential diagnosis is about identifying which of different mental illnesses may best explain the majority (if not all) of a patient's symptoms. This means that the clinician must select one amongst several working (and competing) hypotheses and obviously discard the remaining. Comorbidity, on the other hand, is about asking 'could this patient also have any *additional* mental disorders?' The investigation of additional mental disorders can only take place after a diagnosis is made.

SAQ 4.6

The case formulation conceptualises the patient's current situation. It also organises often intricate and contradictory information about a person, highlighting the dominant patterns that may explain their situation. It includes a hypothesis about the causes and maintaining influences of a person's biological, psychological and social functioning, elaborating on how strengths and impairments in one area may be influencing functioning in another area – highlighting how these complex interactions will be highly specific to individual circumstances. Ideally, the case formulation should serve as a blueprint (or framework) to guide treatment and establish tangible markers to evaluate change, enabling the clinician to follow the patient up. The case formulation is particularly useful in conveying essential information: for example, when reporting the patient to another specialist or back to the family doctor, after psychological assessment and diagnosis.

Comments on activities

Activity 1.1

Strictly speaking, it means 'not normal' in the sense of unusual but this meaning can be problematic. Let's suppose that the frequency of depression increased in the population, so that over 50% of people were suffering from it, would it then have become 'normal'? Rather than percentages of people affected, the usual shade of meaning perhaps has more to do with psychological distress. By this criterion, 'normal' is defined according to the notion that there is a desired ('normal') state of psychological peace of mind. This key issue will be revisited in Chapter 4.

Activity 1.2

Calling an addiction a 'disease' at least suggests bringing sympathy and treatment to addicts rather than moral censure, as in use of the term 'weak-willed'. It is, however, not without its problems: calling Mary's condition a 'disease' risks detracting from the appalling social factors lying behind it and Mary's attempts to use drugs as a solution to her problems. It could prompt a search simply in terms of internal events within Mary's body.

Neha's family argued that she should 'pull herself together'. This reflects the assumption of an element of free will that can overcome distress. Similarly, some people might find it hard to believe that John has a disease and think that if he tried hard enough he could stop his excessive hand-washing. Such an opinion runs counter to the evidence.

Activity 1.3

We would prefer not to arbitrate here but leave this for you to consider in the light of the remainder of SDK228. However, suffice it to say that a rather different way of approaching mental distress is described in the text immediately following this activity. It is an approach that is increasing in popularity.

Activity 1.4

Some suggest that countries with a high level of inequality tend to breed resentment, chronic anger and envy, with an impact on mental ill-health (James, 2007). In addition, large sections of the population might live in conditions that preclude good health, such as high poverty and lack of medical facilities.

Activity 2.1

First, you read the sentence outlining the task. Your brain processed the information in the words, the brain was at the basis of performing the counting and finally the brain organised the command to the muscle controlling the finger to be raised. The brain takes in information in the world, processes it and produces action, in this case in the form of contraction by muscles.

Activity 3.1

It would appear to be classical conditioning. Initially, neutral stimuli (such as the sound of the baby crying) would become conditional stimuli, able to trigger release of oxytocin by virtue of their pairing with suckling. In principle, observations could be made of the capacity of stimuli such as the cry of a baby to trigger oxytocin before suckling first took place. If crying repeatedly came before suckling, then the amount of oxytocin it released would increase over days. Evidence obtained from non-human species under controlled conditions strongly points to such a role of conditioning.

In addition, the sight of the room in which the breastfeeding took place might acquire some conditional capacity to trigger release and thereby come to trigger calming. There are potential health implications here: environments routinely associated with calming could themselves come to *create* calming.

Activity 3.2

You will surely notice a mixture of sad and happy thoughts, optimistic and pessimistic thoughts. At times, thoughts will follow a logical pattern. You might experience some sense that 'you' are in control of your own thoughts (this is termed 'agency'). At other times though, they will just 'pop into your head' apparently from nowhere. Sometimes a thought will grab your attention and not let go despite your best efforts to get away from it. John, the person with OCD from Chapter 1, was an extreme example of this. Other examples are when your mind is dominated by the experience of grief or pain. Perhaps you wish that you had a greater degree of control over your thoughts. You would surely agree that the quality of thoughts is a factor in your subjective well-being.

Activity 4.1

This activity establishes a 'baseline' of what you currently know about this process, to which you will add new information to complement (or challenge) your knowledge as the chapter progresses.

Activity 4.3

Signs: slept very little, worked non-stop, picked a fight, excessive drinking, told everyone about his plans for fame and fortune whilst waiting to be seen by medical staff at the hospital, had slumped shoulders during the interview, monosyllabic, scruffy looking.

Symptoms: mania, delusions ('They're trying to get me'; 'they're talking about me on the telly'), depression, insomnia, isolation (also a sign) and headaches.

Activity 4.5

Has your opinion about diagnosis in mental health changed after reading this chapter? You may be surprised about the far-reaching consequences a mental health diagnosis may have for someone's life. We may be a long way yet from finding a satisfactory method to diagnose patients but in hindsight, it is also possible to take stock of the significant progress that has been made since the Rosenhan experiments in the '70s.

References

APA (2000) *Diagnostic and Statistical Manual of Mental Disorders*, 4th edn, Text Revision (DSM-IV-TR).

Bancroft, J. and Wu, F.C.W. (1983) 'Changes in erectile responsiveness during androgen replacement therapy', *Archives of Sexual Behavior*, vol. 12, pp. 59–66.

Baumeister, R.F. and Leary, M.R. (1995) 'The need to belong: desire for interpersonal attachments as a fundamental human motivation', *Psychological Bulletin*, vol. 117, pp. 497–529.

Baxter, L.R. Jr, Schwartz, J.M., Bergman, K.S, Szuba, M.P., Mazziotta, J.C., Alazrati, A. et al. (1992) 'Caudate glucose metabolic rate changes with both drug and behaviour therapy for obsessive-compulsive disorder', *Archives of General Psychiatry*, vol. 49, pp. 681–9.

Beck, A.T. (2006) *Depression: Causes and Treatment*, Philadelphia, University of Pennsylvania Press.

Beecher, H.K. (1955) 'The powerful placebo', *Journal of the American Medical Association*, vol. 159, pp. 1602–6.

Benedict, R. (1934) 'Anthropology and the abnormal', *Journal of General Psychology*, vol. 10, p. 59.

Berman, M.G., Jonides, J. and Kaplan, S. (2008) 'The cognitive benefits of interacting with nature', *Psychological Science*, vol. 19, pp. 1207–12.

Biver, F., Goldman, S., Francois, A., De La Porte, C., Luxen, A., Gribomont, B. and Lotstra, F. (1995) 'Changes in metabolism of cerebral glucose after stereotaxic leucotomy for refractory obsessive compulsive disorder: a case report', *Journal of Neurology, Neurosurgery and Psychiatry*, vol. 58, pp. 502–5.

Boecker, H., Sprenger, T., Spilker, M.E., Henriksen, G., Koppenhoefer, M., Wagner, K.J. et al. (2008) 'The runner's high: opioidergic mechanisms in the human brain', *Cerebral Cortex*, vol. 18, pp. 2523–31.

Bower, G.H. (1981) 'Mood and memory', *American Psychologist*, vol. 36, pp. 129–48.

Brown, S.L., Brown, R.M., Schiavone, A. and Smith, D.M. (2007) 'Close relationships and health through the lens of selective investment theory', in Post, S. (ed.) *Altruism and Health: Perspectives from Empirical Research*, New York, Oxford University Press, pp. 299–313.

Canino, G. and Alegria, M. (2008) 'Psychiatric diagnosis – is it universal or relative to culture?', *Journal of Child Psychology and Psychiatry*, vol. 49, no. 3, pp. 237–50.

Carver, C.S., Johnson, S.L. and Joormann, J. (2008) 'Serotonergic function, two-mode models of self-regulation, and vulnerability to depression: what depression has in common with impulsive aggression', *Psychological Bulletin*, vol. 134, pp. 912–43.

Coiro, V., Passeri, M., Davoli, C., Bacchi-Modena, A., Bianconi, L., Volpi, R. and Chiodera, P. (1988) 'Oxytocin reduces exercise-induced ACTH and cortisol rise in man', *Acta Endocrinologica (Copenhagen)*, vol. 119, pp. 405–12.

Dalai Lama and Cutler, H.C. (1998) *The Art of Happiness: A Handbook for Living*, Riverhead Books.

Damasio, A.R. (1996) 'The somatic marker hypothesis and the possible functions of the prefrontal cortex', *Philosophical Transactions of the Royal Society of London – Series B: Biological Sciences*, vol. 351, pp. 1413–20.

Danner, D., Snowdon, D.A. and Friesen, W.V. (2001) 'Positive emotions in early life and longevity: findings from the nun study', *Journal of Personality and Social Psychology,* vol. 80, pp. 804–13.

Davidson, R.J. (2005) 'Well-being and affective style: neural substrates and biobehavioural correlates', in Huppert, F.A., Baylis, N. and Keverne, B. (eds) *The Science of Well-Being*, Oxford, Oxford University Press, pp.107–39.

Davidson, R.J. and Fox, N.A. (1989) 'Frontal brain asymmetry predicts infants' response to maternal separation', *Journal of Abnormal Psychology*, vol. 98, pp. 127–31.

Davidson, R.J., Kabat-Zinn, J., Schumacher, J., Rosenkrantz, M., Muller, D., Santorelli, S.F. et al. (2003) 'Alterations in brain and immune function produced by mindfulness meditation', *Psychosomatic Medicine*, vol. 65, pp. 564–70.

Dawson, L. (2008) *Lovesickness and Gender in Early Modern English Literature*, Oxford, Oxford University Press.

Diener, E. (2000) 'Subjective well-being: the science of happiness and a proposal for a national index', *American Psychologist*, vol. 55, pp. 34–43.

Dimsdale, J. and Creed, F. (2009) 'The proposed diagnosis of somatic symptom disorders in DSM-V to replace somatoform disorders in DSM-IV – a preliminary report', *Journal of Psychosomatic Research*, vol. 66, pp. 473–6.

Dishman, K. (1997) 'Brain monoamines, exercise, and behavioural stress: animal models', *Medicine and Science in Sport and Exercise,* vol. 29, pp. 63–74.

Dizon, M., Butler, L.D. and Koopman, C. (2007) 'Befriending man's best friends: does altruism toward animals promote psychological and physical health', in Post, S. (ed.) *Altruism and Health: Perspectives from Empirical Research*, New York, Oxford University Press, pp. 277–91.

Engel, G.L. (1977) 'The need for a new medical model: a challenge for biomedicine', *Science*, vol. 196, pp. 129–36.

Feinstein, A.R. (1970) 'The pre-therapeutic classification of co-morbidity in chronic disease', *Journal of Chronic Disease*, vol. 23, pp. 455–68.

Fuchs, A-R., Ayromlooi, J. and Rasmussen, A.B. (1987) 'Oxytocin response to conditioned and nonconditioned stimuli in lactating ewes', *Biology of Reproduction*, vol. 37, pp. 301–5.

Gilbert, P. and Leahy, R.L. (2009) *The Therapeutic Relationship in the Cognitive Behavioural Psychotherapies*, London, Routledge.

Gratz, K.L. (2003) 'Risk factors for and functions of deliberate self-harm: an empirical and conceptual review', *Clinical Psychology: Science and Practice*, vol. 10, pp. 192–205.

Hammond, D.C. (2005) 'Neurofeedback with anxiety and affective disorders', *Child and Adolescent Psychiatric Clinics of North America*, vol. 14, pp. 105–23.

Heinrichs, M., Baumgartner, T., Kirschbaum, C. and Ehlert, U. (2003) 'Social support and oxytocin interact to suppress cortisol and subjective responses to psychosocial stress', *Biological Psychiatry*, vol. 54, pp. 1389–98.

Hersen, M., Turner, S.M. and Beidel, D.C. (2007) *Adult Psychopathology and Diagnosis* (5th edn), Hoboken, New Jersey, Wiley.

Huppert, F.A., Baylis, N. and Keverne, B. (2005) *The Science of Well-Being*, Oxford, Oxford University Press.

Hwang, W., Myers, H.F., Abe-Kim, J. and Ting, J.Y. (2008) 'A conceptual paradigm for understanding culture's impact on mental health: the cultural influences on mental health (CIMH) model', *Clinical Psychology Review*, vol. 28, pp. 211–27.

Irle, E., Exner, C., Thielen, K., Weninger, G. and Ruther, E. (1998) 'Obsessive-compulsive disorder and ventromedial frontal lesions: clinical and neuropsychological findings', *American Journal of Psychiatry*, vol. 55, pp. 255–63.

James, O. (2007) 'Selfish capitalism and mental illness', *The Psychologist*, vol. 20, pp. 426–8.

Janal, M.N., Colt, E.W.D., Clark, W.C. and Glusman, M. (1984) 'Pain sensitivity, mood and plasma endocrine levels in man following long-distance running: effects of naloxone', *Pain*, vol. 19, pp. 13–25.

Jevning, R., Wallace, R.K. and Beidebach, M. (1992) 'The physiology of meditation: a review. A wakeful hypometabolic integrated response', *Neuroscience and Biobehavioral Reviews*, vol. 16, pp. 415–24.

Kaplan, S. (1995) 'The restorative benefits of nature: toward an integrative framework', *Journal of Environmental Psychology*, vol. 15, pp. 169–82.

Kaplan, S. (2001) 'Meditation, restoration, and the management of mental fatigue', *Environment and Behavior*, vol. 33, pp. 480–506.

Kasser, T. (2002) *The High Price of Materialism*, Cambridge, The MIT Press.

Kessler, R.C., McGonagle, K.A., Zhao, S., Nelson, C.B., Hughes, M., Eshlema, S. et al. (1994) 'Lifetime and 12-month prevalence of DSM-III-R psychiatric disorders in the United States: results from the National Comorbidity Survey', *Archives of General Psychiatry*, vol. 51, pp. 8–19.

Kessler, R.C.; Berglund, P., Demler, O., Jin, R., Merikangas, K.R., Walters, E.E. et al. (2005) 'Lifetime prevalence and age-of-onset distributions of DSM-IV disorders in the national comorbidity survey replication'. *Archives of General Psychiatry*, vol. 62, 593–602.

Kosfeld, M., Heinrichs, M., Zak, P.J., Fischbacher, U. and Fehr, E. (2005) 'Oxytocin increases trust in humans', *Nature*, vol. 435, pp. 673–6.

Lewis, G. and Wilkinson, G. (1993) 'Another British disease? A recent increase in the prevalence of psychiatric morbidity', *Journal of Epidemiology and Community Health*, vol. 47, pp. 358–61.

Loring, M. and Powell, B. (1988) 'Gender, race, and DSM-III: a study of objectivity of psychiatric diagnostic behavior', *Journal of Health and Social Behavior*, vol. 29, pp. 1–22.

Lutz, A., Slagter, H.A., Dunne, J.D. and Davidson, R.J. (2008) 'Cognitive-emotional interactions – attention regulation and monitoring in meditation', *Trends in Cognitive Sciences*, vol. 12, pp. 163–9.

Maj, M. (2005) 'Psychiatric comorbidity': an artefact of current diagnostic systems?, *British Journal of Psychiatry*, vol. 186, pp. 182–4.

Marks, N. and Shah, H. (2005) 'A well-being manifesto for a flourishing society', in Huppert, F. A., Baylis, N. and Keverne, B. (eds) *The Science of Well-Being*, Oxford, Oxford University Press, pp. 503–31.

Marques, A.H. and Sternberg, E.M. (2007) 'The biology of positive emotions and health', in Post, S. (ed.) *Altruism and Health: Perspectives from Empirical Research*, New York, Oxford University Press, pp. 149–88.

McNeilly, A.S., Robinson, I.C.A.F., Houston, M.J. and Howie, P.W. (1983) 'Release of oxytocin and prolactin in response to suckling', *British Medical Journal*, vol. 286, pp. 257–9.

Mezzich, J.E. (2002) 'International surveys on the use of ICD-10 and related diagnostic systems', *Psychopathology* vol. 35, no. 2–3, pp. 72–5.

Moreno, C., Laje, G., Blanco, C., Jiang, H., Schmidt, A.B. and Olfson, M. (2007) 'National trends in the outpatient diagnosis and treatment of bipolar disorder in youth', *Archives of General Psychiatry*, vol. 64, no. 9, pp. 1032–9.

Morgan, W.P (1985) 'Affective beneficence of vigorous physical activity', *Medicine and Science in Sports and Exercise*, vol. 17, pp. 94–100.

Morrison, J. (2007) *Diagnosis Made Easier: Principles and Techniques for Mental Health Clinicians*, New York, Guilford Press.

Newberg, A.B. and Iversen, J. (2003) 'The neural basis of the complex mental task of meditation: neurotransmitter and neurochemical considerations', *Medical Hypotheses*, vol. 61, pp. 282–91.

Odendaal, J.S.J. and Meintjes, R.A. (2003) 'Neurophysiological correlates of affiliative behaviour between humans and dogs', *The Veterinary Journal*, vol. 165, pp. 296–301.

Okasha, A., Saad, A., Khalil, A.H., Seif El Dawla, A. and Yehia, N. (1994) 'Phenomenology of obsessive–compulsive disorder: a transcultural study', *Comprehensive Psychiatry*, vol. 35, pp. 191–7.

Oman, D. (2007) 'Does volunteering foster physical health and longevity?', in Post, G. (ed.) *Altruism and Health: Perspectives from Empirical Research*, New York, Oxford University Press, pp. 15–32.

Orme-Johnson, D.W., Schneider, R.H., Son, Y.D., Nidich, S. and Cho, Z-H. (2006) 'Neuroimaging of meditation's effect on brain reactivity to pain', *Neuroreport*, vol. 17, pp. 1359–63.

Otto, M.W., Church, T.S., Craft, L.L., Greer, T.L., Smits, J.A.J. and Trivedi, M.H. (2007) 'Exercise for mood and anxiety disorders', *Journal of Clinical Psychiatry*, vol. 68, pp. 1–8.

Panksepp, J. (1998) *Affective Neuroscience*, New York, Oxford University Press.

Paquette, V., Lévesque, J., Mensour, B., Leroux, J-M., Beaudoin, G., Bourgouin, P. and Beauregard, M. (2003) '"Change your mind and you change the brain": effects of cognitive-behavioral therapy on the neural correlates of spider phobia', *NeuroImage*, vol. 18, pp. 401–9.

Paul, K.I., Geithner, E. and Moser, K. (2009) 'Latent deprivation among people who are employed, unemployed, or out of the labour force', *Journal of Psychology*, vol. 143, pp. 477–91.

Peterson, C., Seligman, M.E.P. and Vaillant, G.E. (1988) 'Pessimistic explanatory style is a risk factor for physical illness: a thirty-five-year longitudinal study', *Journal of Personality and Social Psychology*, vol. 55, pp. 23–7.

Pickett, K.E., James, O.W. and Wilkinson, R.G. (2009) 'Income inequality and the prevalence of mental illness: a preliminary international analysis', *Journal of Epidemiology and Community Health*, vol. 60, pp. 646–7.

Pincus, H.A., Frances, A., Davis, W.W., First, M.B. and Widiger, T.A. (1992) 'DSM-IV and new diagnostic categories: holding the line on proliferation', *American Journal of Psychiatry*, vol. 149, pp. 112–17.

Post, S.G. (2007) *Altruism and Health: Perspectives from Empirical Research*, New York, Oxford University Press.

Rash, C.J., Coffey, S.F., Baschnagel, J.S., Drobes, D.J. and Saladin, M.E. (2008) 'Psychometric properties of the IES-R in traumatized substance dependent individuals with and without PTSD', *Addictive Behaviour*, vol. 33, no. 8, pp. 1039–47.

Reinarman, C. and Levine, H.G. (1997) *Crack in America: Demon Drugs and Social Justice*, Berkeley, University of California Press.

Rosenhan, D.L. (1973) 'On being sane in insane places', *Science*, vol. 179, no. 407, pp. 250–8.

Rounsaville, B.J., Kosten, T.R., Williams, J.B. and Spitzer, R.L. (1987) 'A field trial of DSM-III-R psychoactive substance dependence disorders', *American Journal of Psychiatry*, vol. 144, pp. 351–5.

Saha, S., Chant, D.C., Welham, J.L. and McGrath, J.J. (2006) 'The incidence and prevalence of schizophrenia varies with latitude', *Acta Psychiatrica Scandinavica*, vol. 114, pp. 36–9.

Salkovskis, P.M. (1999) 'Understanding and treating obsessive–compulsive disorder', *Behaviour Research and Therapy*, vol. 37, S29–S52.

Sandman, C.A., Hetrick, W., Taylor, D.V., Marion, S.D., Touchette, P., Barron, J.L. et al. (2000) 'Long-term effects of naltrexone on self-injurious behavior', *American Journal of Mental Retardation*, vol. 105, no. 2, pp. 103–17.

Schneider, R.H., Staggers, F., Alexander, C.N., Sheppard, W., Rainforth, M., Kondwani, K. et al. (1995) 'A randomized controlled trial of stress reduction for hypertension in older African Americans', *Hypertension*, vol. 26, pp. 820–7.

Schwartz, J. (1996) *Brain Lock: Free Yourself from Obsessive–Compulsive Behavior*, London, HarperCollins.

Siegel, S. (2005) 'Drug tolerance, drug addiction, and drug anticipation', *Current Directions in Psychological Science*, vol. 14, pp. 296–300.

Slater, L. (2004) *Opening Skinner's Box: Great Psychological Experiments of the Twentieth Century*, New York, Norton.

Smits, J.A.J., Berry, A.C., Rosenfield, D., Powers, M.B., Behar, E. and Otto, M.W. (2008) 'Reducing anxiety sensitivity with exercise', *Depression and Anxiety*, vol. 25, pp. 689–99.

Sobotka, S.S., Davidson, R.J. and Senulis, J.A. (1992) 'Anterior brain electrical asymmetries in response to reward and punishment', *Electroencephalography and Clinical Neurophysiology*, vol. 83, pp. 236–47.

Stewart-Williams, S. and Podd, J. (2004) 'The placebo effect: dissolving the expectancy versus conditioning debate', *Psychological Bulletin*, vol. 130, pp. 324–40.

Szasz, T.S. (1973) *The Second Sin*, New York, Anchor/Doubleday, p. 113.

Szasz, T. (1994) *Cruel Compassion: Psychiatry's Control of Society's Unwanted*, New York, Wiley.

Tang, Y-Y., Ma, Y., Wang, J., Fan, Y., Feng, S., Lu, Q. et al. (2007) 'Short-term meditation training improves attention and self-regulation', *Proceedings of the National Academy of Sciences*, vol. 104, pp. 17152–6.

Temerlin, M.K. (1970) 'Diagnostic bias in community mental health', *Community Mental Health Journal*, vol. 6, pp. 110–17.

Toates, F. (1995) *Stress: Conceptual and Biological Aspects*, Chichester, Wiley.

Toates, F. (2010) 'Understanding drug treatments: a biopsychosocial approach', in Barker, M., Vossler, A. and Langdridge, D. (eds) *Understanding Counselling and Psychotherapy*, London, Sage Publications, pp. 45–75.

Uno, H., Tarara, R., Else, J.G., Suleman, M.A. and Sapolsky, R.M. (1989) 'Hippocampal damage associated with prolonged and fatal stress in primates', *Journal of Neuroscience*, vol. 9, pp. 1705–11.

Uvnäs-Moberg, K. (1998) 'Antistress pattern induced by oxytocin', *News in Physiological Sciences*, vol. 13, pp. 22–6.

Uvnäs-Moberg, K., Arn, I. and Magnusson, D. (2005) 'The psychobiology of emotion: the role of the oxytocinergic system', *International Journal of Behavioral Medicine*, vol. 12, pp. 59–65.

Wenk-Sormaz, H. (2005) 'Meditation can reduce habitual responding', *Alternative Therapies in Health and Medicine*, vol. 11, pp. 42–58.

WHO (1994) *The International Statistical Classification of Diseases and Related Health Problems*, 10th revision (ICD-10).

Williams, R. (1989) *The Trusting Heart*, New York, Times Books.

Zak, P.J., Kurzban, R. and Matzner, W.T. (2005) 'Oxytocin is associated with human trustworthiness', *Hormones and Behavior*, vol. 48, pp. 522–7.

Zhong, C-B. and Liljenquist, K. (2006) 'Washing away your sins: threatened morality and physical cleansing', *Science*, vol. 313, pp. 1451–2.

Acknowledgements

Grateful acknowledgement is made to the following sources:

Tables

Table 1.1: © Okasha, A. et al. (1994) 'Common themes of obsession in Egypt, India, England and Jerusalem', *Comprehensive Psychiatry*, vol. 35, Elsevier Science.

Figures

Figure 1.1: © Courtesy of Crown Copyright FERA/Science Photo Library; Figure 1.2: © Bluestone/Science Photo Library; Figure 1.3: © Chris Laurens/ Alamy; Figure 1.4: © AJ Photo/Science Photo Library; Figure 1.5: © Conor Caffrey/Science Photo Library; Figure 1.6: © amana images inc./Alamy; Figure 1.7: © David Levenson/Alamy; Figure 1.10: Pickett, K.E. et al. (2006), 'Income inequality and prevalence of mental illness', *Journal of Epidemiology and Community Health,* BMJ Publishing Group; Figure 2.7: Courtesy www. wellsphere.com; Figure 2.8: © Horne J. (1988) *Why We Sleep*, Reprinted by permission of Oxford University Press; Figure 2.9a: CC Studio/Science Photo Library; Figure 2.9b: WELLCOME Dept of Cognitive Neurology/Science Photo Library; Figure 2.10: © Silbersweig D.A. et al. (1995) 'A functional neuroanatomy of hallucinations in schizophrenia', *Nature*, vol. 378, Nature Publishing Co.; Figure 2.11: © Martini, F.H., Timmons, M.J. and McKinley, M.P. (2000) *Human Anatomy*; Figure 2.12: Toates, F. (2001) 'The brain of several mammalian species showing the prefrontal cortex', *Biological Psychology*, Elsevier Science; Figure 2.13: Toates, F. (2001) 'PET scans of control and OCD brain', *Biological Psychology*, Elsevier Science; Figure 2.14: © Baxter et al. (1992), 'Caudate glucose metabolic rate changes with both drug and behaviour therapy in OCD', *Archives of General Psychiatry*, American Medical Association; Figure 2.15a: © Toates, F., (2001), 'Motor action by a finger triggered by a conscious decision in the brain', *Biological Psychology*, Elsevier Science; Figure 2.23: © Toates, F. (2001) 'How transmitter is removed from the synaptic cleft', *Biological Psychology*, Elsevier Science; Figure 2.24: Toates, F. (2001) 'The action of a drug on blocking reuptake', *Biological Psychology*, Elsevier Science; Figure 2.25: Toates, F. (2001) 'A drug that targets a natural neurotransmitter and the side effect', *Biological Psychology*, Elsevier Science; Figure 2.29: Toates, F. (2001) 'Classification of (classical) neurotransmitters and hormones', *Biological Psychology*, Elsevier Science; Figure 2.31: Toates, F. (2001), 'Part of the somatic nervous system and part of the ANS', *Biological Psychology*, Elsevier Science; Figure 3.2: Adapted from Kalat J.W. (1998), 'The sympathetic nervous system and parasympathetic nervous system', *Biological Psychology*, 6th edn, Brooks; Figure 3.6: © Smits et al. (2008) 'Reducing anxiety sensitivity with exercise', *Anxiety & Depression*; Figure 3.10: © Heinrichs M. et al. (2003) 'Social support and oxytocin interact to suppress cortisol and subjective responses to psychosocial stress', *Biological Psychiatry*; Figure 3.12: © McNeilly, A.S. et al. (1983) *British Medical Journal*; Figure 3.13: © Nature Publishing Group (2005), Kosfeld, M. et al. (2005)

SDK228 Team

Claire Rostron (*SDK228 Chair and Academic Editor*)
Viki Burnage (*SDK228 Manager*)
Helen Copperwheat (*SDK228 Assistant*)
Fred Toates (*Block 1 Chair*)
Antonio Martins-Mourao
Saroj Datta (*Block 2 Chair*)
Heather McLannahan (*SDK228 Deputy Chair*)
Ellie Dommett (*Block 3 Chair*)
Katherine Leys (*Block 4 Chair*)

Consultants

Ilona Boniwell
Christine Heading
Margaret Swithenby

External assessor

Professor Neil Frude

Critical readers

Meg Barker
Mick McCormick
Ulf Wagner

Developmental testers

Elena Gammage
Jen Evans
Vicky Gaeta

Production team

Greg Black
Ann Carter
Martin Chiverton
Roger Courthold
Rebecca Graham
Sara Hack
Nicky Heath
Chris Hough
Carol Houghton
Roger Moore
Jon Owen
Judith Pickering
Brian Richardson
Federica Sacco
Bina Sharma

Indexer

Jane Henley

Library

Duncan Belks

Index

Index entries and page numbers in **bold** are glossary terms. Page numbers in *italics* refer to figures or tables.